TWENTY TURBULENT YEARS

THE TRANSFORMATION OF BRITAIN'S BUS INDUSTRY

1980–2000

PETER ROWLANDS and STEWART J. BROWN

fawndoon

Twenty Turbulent Years
First published by Fawndoon Books 2022
ISBN 978-0-9934831-5-8
© Peter Rowlands and Stewart J. Brown 2022

Photographs by Peter Rowlands

Designed by Helen Swansbourne
Printed by Gomer Press

Also published by Fawndoon Books
Scotland's Buses in the 1960s (2016)
Advancing in a Forward Direction (2017)
Glasgow's Buses (2018)
London's Bus Purchases 1946–1994 (2019)

www.fawndoon.com
www.peterrowlands.com

FRONT COVER: Between 1994 and 1997 Maidstone &
District bought 33 Volvo Olympians with Northern
Counties bodies of a style variously known as the
Palatine or the Countybus. Maidstone & District's
buses had been a sombre dark green until the start
of the 1970s when they became leaf green under
NBC's corporate diktat. This bright livery adopted
by the privatised company honoured the company's
tradition, but in an exciting new way.

BACK COVER: *Top*, seen in 1980, when it was 14 years
old, a 70-seat Bristol Lodekka FLF6G of Eastern
Counties passes a slightly older 60-seat FS5G in
Norwich. *Bottom*, in 2000 a MkII MCW Metrobus of
Travel West Midlands, then 16 years old, is seen in
Birmingham.

ENDPAPERS: Seen in 2000, an Optare Spectra new to
Travel West Midlands in 1999, and in 1981, a Greater
Manchester Leyland PD2 new to Wigan Corporation
in 1966.

OPPOSITE: A Chesterfield Transport Roe-bodied Leyland
Fleetline passes the town's most famous landmark,
St Mary and All Saints church with its crooked spire.
When this bus was delivered in 1978 Chesterfield
was among a declining number of urban operators
specifying dual-door buses. The 1978 Fleetlines were
Chesterfield Transport's last new double-deckers; its
next, bought in 1980–81, were ex-London Transport
Fleetlines. This is a 1987 view.

Contents

1
Introduction

There were just over 200 half-cab double-deckers in service in local authority fleets in 1980, most of them Leyland Titans or AEC Regents. Among the latter was this 1963 bus in the Ipswich Borough Transport fleet. It had 65-seat bodywork by Neepsend and is arriving in the bus station used by the town's municipal buses. Town-bound buses showed Electric House as their destination rather than the more prosaic Bus Station. Electric House, located opposite the western end of the bus station, had been the offices of Ipswich Corporation's electricity department.

◄ In 1980 the buses operated by the South Yorkshire PTE were painted in a bland cream livery with light brown relief. In 1990 PTE-owned South Yorkshire Transport was using this bright colour scheme with Mainline as the fleetname – a radical transformation. This Mark II MCW Metrobus was one of 20 delivered to the PTE in 1984. It is loading in central Sheffield.

In 1980 the vast majority of buses in Great Britain were in public ownership. Twenty years later, virtually all of them were run by the private sector. The Conservative government of the early 1980s was determined to step back from involvement in public services, and the bus industry proved an easy target.

It was a massive transformation, and in the course of it the industry went through a long, sometimes painful, upheaval. Newly-independent regional and local bus companies blossomed and then merged into bigger groups. Local authority bus ownership, still a major component of the industry in 1980, shrunk steadily as the government encouraged councils to sell their bus operations.

Competition, still an alien concept in the bus world of 1980, came to the fore as 50 years of regulation of bus services was brought to an end; and in some cases the outcome was dramatic. Buses jostled for customers in over-trafficked streets. Minibuses briefly flooded the market.

Even London, traditionally regarded as a special case in Britain's bus world, saw massive change. London Transport's bus operations were first divisionalised and then privatised, although a form of route tendering that was unique in the UK ensured that service provision stayed in public control.

The wind of change was also felt in bus manufacturing. In 1980, Leyland was still the market leader by a long way, despite recent missteps such as its attempt to foist its integral Titan double-decker on a reluctant market. By 2000, Leyland had faded away and so, too, had Metro-Cammell Weymann, which for a while had been one of Leyland's main rivals. An unexpected successor for the role of bus market leader was emerging in the shape of Dennis,

which, after a series of ownership changes, emerged in 2000 as part of TransBus International.

All this was certainly unsettling, but on the street it was also invigorating. As privatisation unfolded in the 1980s, some old bus company names were revived and new ones emerged. Striking new liveries were developed – some remarkably stylish, others clearly developed in haste.

The change of identity was especially evident in the National Bus Company, with its regional subsidiaries spread across England and Wales. For more than ten years these had been virtually hidden behind a uniform public face and bland red or green colour schemes. Suddenly the individual constituents of the organisation re-emerged, as if expanding from two dimensions into three.

Surviving local authority operators also launched new identities, keen to share in the resurgence of interest in the way buses *looked* as well as how they performed. This trend reached its zenith in the period from the mid-1980s to the mid-1990s. The bus world of that period seemed arresting and dynamic, with a strong emphasis on presentation and local identity. On the surface, it appeared to realise the dreams of the free-market politicians who had made it all happen.

What was less obvious to the casual observer was the loss of subsidy for unprofitable routes and the withdrawal of services in evenings and at weekends. Meanwhile, the revived independence in the bus world gradually faded as newly-emerging bus groups bought out individual companies. By 2000 it was clear that they had become the future of the industry; and with notable exceptions, their rigidly-imposed corporate identities underlined the disappearance of the enterprising spirit that had briefly flourished across the market.

DEREGULATION

PROBLEM? OPPORTUNITY?

OPTARE
have cracked it!

➤ In 1980 nobody could have predicted that Dennis would emerge as Britain's biggest bus builder in the 1990s. Its success was down to one model, the Dart midibus. The original step-entrance model, introduced in 1989, was replaced by the low-floor Dart SLF in 1996. The most popular body on the Dart in the 1990s was the Plaxton Pointer, as seen on this 1997 bus for British Bus subsidiary Stevensons of Uttoxeter. It was photographed in Burton-on-Trent when new with branding for service 8.

Meanwhile a lot was happening on the world stage. In some ways the period between 1980 and 2000 bridges the gap between the relatively recent past and what now looks like increasingly distant history. Still to come at the start of the period were the UK miners' strike, the Falklands war, the fall of the Soviet Union, the Gulf war. Still alive in 1980 were Graham Greene, Alfred Hitchcock, John Lennon, Harold Macmillan, Peter Sellers. And Ronald Reagan had not even started his eight-year term as US President.

In 1980 the internet was unknown to the vast majority of people; its widespread household use only dates back to the mid-1990s. Yet by 2000 it was an established fact of life. In 1980 there were no mobile phones; by 2000 they were commonplace, although today's smartphone was still nearly a decade away. In some of the photographs in this book you may see people who appear to be checking their email on their phone, but don't be fooled. They were probably consulting a printed bus timetable or reading a book.

In 1980 you could often recognise the town or city you were in simply from its buses, which had their own distinctive liveries and bore fleetnames that proudly announced their local ownership. By 2000 this was largely a thing of the past. With notable exceptions, buses operated by the groups that dominated the industry looked more or less the same wherever you went.

The two authors of *Twenty Turbulent Years* have both been closely engaged with the bus industry. The idea came from Peter Rowlands, a transport industry writer and editor, and more recently a mystery novelist with half a dozen titles to his name. He was an avid bus photographer throughout the period covered by this book, and took all the photographs in it. He has also contributed a chapter on liveries and added occasional insights elsewhere.

Stewart Brown, a long-time passenger transport editor, journalist and photographer in his own right, has joined forces with Peter to retell the story of that turbulent time. He makes full use of his encyclopaedic knowledge of the bus industry, presenting a complex story in a clear, engaging style, and augmenting the narrative with a fascinating array of charts and graphical material.

Peter remembers the period as one of constant frenzied activity, in which he wanted to be everywhere at once, and to photograph everything of note in the bus world. He willingly acknowledges that this was an impossible aim; but as this book attests, he managed to capture much of the spirit of the era with photographs that cover the country and span the whole period. Very few of those appearing in this book have been published before.

Clearly it would have been impossible to cover every nuance of this extraordinary story in a single book. The saga of the NBC sell-off alone would warrant several volumes. Instead, our objective has been to record the main developments during the period and convey the flavour of the time, using a combination of informative prose and striking photography.

To keep the story even half-way manageable, the scope has been limited to Great Britain, which embraces England, Scotland and Wales but not Northern Ireland; and we have focused mainly on buses rather than coaches, though we have included various key coaching developments to help flesh out the wider context of the story.

We are indebted to Gavin Booth for reading the proofs and making invaluable suggestions, and as always at Fawndoon we are grateful to Helen Swansbourne for applying her graphic design flair to make this book visually so enticing. Needless to say, any errors are purely our own.

It is hard to look back on this period without a trace of regret – not just because it is a part of our lives we won't have again, but also because so much was lost in the bus industry in terms of variety, visual exuberance, and affordable services. Some might say the dispersed nature of the industry at the start of the period, combined with the artificial constraints imposed by rigid service regulation, meant that inefficiency was endemic. On the other hand, it is equally arguable that the ensuing era of competition ultimately brought more benefits to operators than it did to the passengers they were there to serve, and the progressive withdrawal of subsidy left many people who once enjoyed regular bus provision without it.

Whichever view you take, we hope you enjoy revisiting a period that still seems recent to us, but which is rapidly dwindling in the memory – becoming at the same time brighter and more distant.

Stewart J. Brown
Largs, 2022

Peter Rowlands
Fulham, 2022

How local control gave way to big-group dominance in Britain's largest cities

CITY	1980 OPERATOR	2000 OPERATOR
Aberdeen	Grampian Region	First
Birmingham	West Midlands PTE	National Express
Bradford	West Yorkshire PTE	First
Bristol	NBC: Bristol Omnibus	First
Cambridge	NBC: Eastern Counties	Stagecoach
Canterbury	NBC: East Kent	Stagecoach
Cardiff	Local authority	Local authority
Carlisle	NBC: Ribble	Stagecoach
Coventry	West Midlands PTE	National Express
Derby	Local authority	Arriva
Dundee	Tayside Region	National Express
Edinburgh	Lothian Region	Local authority
Exeter	NBC: Devon General	Stagecoach
Glasgow	Strathclyde PTE	First
Gloucester	NBC: Bristol Omnibus	Stagecoach
Hull	Local authority	Stagecoach
Lancaster	Local authority	Stagecoach
Leeds	West Yorkshire PTE	First
Leicester	Local authority	First
Liverpool	Merseyside PTE	Arriva
Manchester	Greater Manchester PTE	First/Stagecoach
Newcastle	Tyne & Wear PTE	Stagecoach
Norwich	NBC: Eastern Counties	First
Nottingham	Local authority	Local authority
Oxford	NBC: City of Oxford	Go-Ahead
Peterborough	NBC: Eastern Counties	Stagecoach
Plymouth	Local authority	Local authority
Portsmouth	Local authority	First
Preston	Local authority	MBO
Salford	Greater Manchester PTE	First
Sheffield	South Yorkshire PTE	First
Southampton	Local authority	First
Stoke-on-Trent	NBC: Potteries	First
Sunderland	Tyne & Wear PTE	Stagecoach
Swansea	NBC: South Wales	First
Wakefield	NBC: West Riding	Arriva
Winchester	NBC: Hants & Dorset	Stagecoach
Wolverhampton	West Midlands PTE	National Express
Worcester	NBC: Midland Red	First
York	NBC: York-West Yorkshire	First

This chart shows how local or regional ownership and identity dwindled among the buses of Britain's 40 largest cities between 1980 and 2000. At the start of the period the major operators in 25 of these cities were in local or regional ownership with their own identities (shown in colour in the chart), and only 15 belonged to a large group – the National Bus Company – with a nationwide identity. By the end of the period the number of cities served by a nationwide group with a corporate identity – Arriva, First and Stagecoach – had doubled from 15 to 30.

Key

 Cities whose main operator had a local or regional identity

Cities whose main operator had a corporate national identity

2
All change!

Over the years many small operators favoured Bedfords for both coach and bus operation. In 1987 Mervyn's Coaches of Micheldever was running this 1974 YRQ with Duple Dominant body, seen in Winchester ready to return to its base on a service introduced in 1986 at the start of deregulation. The coach had been new to Battersby-Silver Grey of Morecambe. Behind it is a bronze statue of King Arthur, who is traditionally associated with the city.

I n 1980 Britain's bus industry was in a situation which could best be described as stable decline. The number of people travelling by bus had been falling steadily for 30 years. On the other hand the country's coach industry was on the verge of remarkable expansion, thanks to the government's policy of deregulating express services and tours, opening up the market to anyone who wanted to have a go.

The bulk of the country's local bus services were operated by public sector organisations. Between them the National Bus Company, London Transport, the Scottish Bus Group, seven passenger transport executives and 49 municipal fleets ran almost 42,000 buses and coaches, as recorded in the 1980 fleet survey published by *Commercial Motor*:

OPERATING SECTOR	FLEET
NBC	15,538
PTE	10,479
London	6,475
Municipal	5,631
SBG	3,718
TOTAL	**41,841**

There were a number of independent operators running bus services. Most were small family-run firms serving small towns and rural areas. There were clusters of independents operating around Durham, Paisley and central Ayrshire. The last surviving large independent, Barton Transport of Nottingham, ran a fleet of just over 200 vehicles, but most of the independents owned fewer than 20.

The nation's bus fleets had been modernised in the 1970s, thanks in part to government support for most of the decade in the form of a 50 per cent grant towards the cost of a new bus. This had been introduced to speed the adoption of one-person operation to reduce costs and address the perennial problem of a shortage of drivers and

▲ Ayrshire had a long history of independent bus operation, and this 1991 view in Irvine shows the two best-known names, A1 and AA. The A1 bus is a 1975 Alexander-bodied Ailsa which had been new to Maidstone & District. It was purchased by A1 in 1984, where it joined a number of similar buses bought new. In the background are two AA Leyland Nationals. Both operations were taken over by Stagecoach later in the 1990s.

▼ Barton Transport was one of Britain's biggest independent operators and in the 1970s had used the government's new bus grant to fund a massive fleet renewal, buying some 400 Leylands and Bedfords with coach bodies by Plaxton and Duple. The two-piece power-operated doors on this Leopard were part of the bus grant specification. When new in 1974 it had high-backed coach seats. This is Nottingham in 1990, shortly after the Barton business had been purchased by Wellglade, the owners of Trent.

◀ In 1980 the biggest fleet of half-cab buses in Britain was to be found in London, where Routemasters made up just over 40 per cent of the 6,475-strong London Transport bus fleet. This is a 1987 view of a Routemaster which had been new in 1962 and would survive in service in London until 2004. Route 159, latterly running between Streatham Station and Marble Arch, was the last regular service to be operated by Routemasters, being converted to one-person operation in 2005.

conductors. It also hastened the demise of the traditional half-cab double-decker. In 1980 there were just under a thousand still in service outside London, but only 20 years before that virtually all double-deckers had been of this layout. Most of the survivors were Bristol Lodekkas, some 600 of which were running for NBC and SBG, though a smattering of other makes could also be found in isolated pockets. But in London there were almost 2,800 Routemasters, making up just over 40 per cent of the London Transport fleet and highlighting just how far out of step LT was with the rest of the country. Or, if you're a Londoner, how far out of step the rest of the country was with LT.

The transport industry's first taste of deregulation came with the abolition in 1980 of the licensing system which for 50 years had controlled express services, excursions and tours. Most observers would agree that it was a resounding success. In the years following coach deregulation fares came down, service frequencies improved, journey times were reduced and, spurred on by the competition they were facing, both National Express and SBG's Scottish Citylink introduced new high-quality coaches, including double-deckers to provide more capacity. Passengers benefited. The coach industry benefited. The main loser was British Rail.

◄ One of the most significant developments of the 1980s was the widespread introduction of minibuses on high-frequency urban services. The biggest user was the National Bus Company, and the pioneering operator was Devon General, which took delivery of 162 Ford Transits in 1986. Four with 16-seat Carlyle bodies and Bayline branding are seen in Torbay in the summer of 1988 after Devon General had been privatised in a management buy-out.

Some smaller coach operators also tried to take advantage of the opportunities presented by deregulation, though most initiatives were fairly short-lived. That includes the high-profile British Coachways consortium, which tried to challenge the virtual monopoly of NBC's National Express network in England and Wales, but which lasted just two years.

Local bus deregulation followed in 1986, but here even the most ardent supporter of free enterprise would surely accept that the results were at best patchy. In all the big conurbations outside London the PTEs faced competition from a myriad of new operators, most of whom at the start were running second-hand buses with varying degrees of professionalism. There were fleet reductions among the PTEs, with the biggest cuts coming at Greater Manchester where over 450 assorted buses – roughly 20 per cent of the fleet – were withdrawn and sold in 1986 in an effort to make the organisation leaner and better equipped for what was to come. Some of these buses were then used by new operators to compete with the PTE.

Fleets of minibuses were pressed in to service by many major operators. Some were a response to competition, others were used as a way of discouraging would-be competitors. Between 1984 and 1986 NBC bought around 4,000 minibuses. The early van-based vehicles were fairly crude but they were cheap to buy, proved to be more durable than anybody expected, led to imaginative marketing initiatives and – most importantly for users – significantly improved frequencies on many busy urban services.

Most established operators responded well to deregulation. But on top of that, the government wanted to reduce public sector involvement in the running of local buses, creating yet another challenge for bus company managers, who now had to prepare for privatisation. As a prelude to this, NBC split up some of its biggest companies in the early 1980s, initially to create stronger locally-

▲ There was particularly intense competition in and around Glasgow when local bus services were deregulated in 1986. But there were some skirmishes beforehand, notably when Scottish Bus Group subsidiary Central Scottish took advantage of a relaxation in the licensing regulations to combine existing services to create new cross-city links. This Alexander-bodied Dennis Dominator was one of 20 delivered in 1981 and is seen in the city centre in 1984 on a service from East Kilbride in the south-east to Duntocher in the north-west.

◄ Deregulation saw significant reductions in most PTE fleets. As well as withdrawing time-expired buses, Greater Manchester disposed of some relatively young non-standard types, including its 15 Leyland Titans. Five were purchased by newly-privatised NBC subsidiary South Midland in 1987, including this eight-year-old bus arriving in Oxford with its destination set for the return trip to Bicester. Its unusual and arresting livery replaced the privatised company's initial more muted maroon and white, illustrated on page 21.

managed businesses, but later to create companies which would not dominate local markets and would be more attractive to prospective buyers. Then between 1986 and 1988 the subsidiaries of what had once claimed to be the biggest bus and coach operator in the world were sold off, company by company. Most were bought by their management teams.

There were direct parallels in Scotland. In 1985 SBG reorganised its subsidiaries to create eleven bus-operating companies where previously there had been seven. This created companies whose operating areas were more closely aligned with the boundaries of the regional councils. Following the privatisation of NBC the government then announced that SBG, too, was to be privatised. The Group's management, backed by most of its employees, wanted to see it privatised as a single entity, but that didn't happen. As at NBC, each company was sold separately.

The government also encouraged the PTEs and local authorities to sell off their bus operations, and in order to facilitate this, the 1985 Transport Act required these to be set up as so-called arm's length companies. The seven PTEs' bus companies were privatised between 1988 and 1994, sometimes with a measure of acrimony as the ideology of Conservative central government clashed with that of the generally Labour-leaning passenger transport authorities which oversaw the PTEs.

The fates of the 49 municipal fleets varied. Their operators were not legally obliged to dispose of them, but some of the smallest simply collapsed in the face of fierce competition, and others were acquired in management-led employee buy-outs. Some of these lasted only a short time before the resultant privatised business was bought by one of the emerging new groups – British Bus, Badgerline, Stagecoach, and GRT. Some others were purchased directly by these groups. By 2000 only 17 of the original 49 local authority bus fleets remained in public sector ownership.

The government repeatedly promised deregulation for London, but this never happened. As early as 1985 London Regional Transport introduced a form of competition in the shape of route tendering, and this was meant to be just a first step towards opening up the market further. However, faced with the upheaval and widely acknowledged decline in service levels in other major conurbations, the government eventually abandoned the idea of deregulation for London, opting instead to continue with the programme of route tendering. This saw new operators – both independents and NBC subsidiaries – winning a significant number of contracts at the expense of London Buses. Tendering introduced a colourful period in London's transport history before LRT insisted in 1997 that buses used on contracted services should be painted predominantly red.

The growth of the new bus groups was dramatic. Looking purely at the groups' British operations, Badgerline started out in 1986 as a management buy-out of an NBC company running 400 buses; by 1995, when it merged with GRT to form FirstBus, it was running 4,000 vehicles. GRT had been formed in 1989 and was running 1,600 vehicles when it merged with Badgerline. By 2000 the First fleet in Britain numbered 10,000 buses and coaches.

In 1987–88 Drawlane bought four NBC companies running just over 1,000 buses. It was reformed as British Bus in 1992 and was running 5,600 buses when it was taken over by Cowie in 1996. Perhaps the most remarkable of the new groups was Stagecoach, which started running express coaches in Scotland in 1980 and 20 years later was operating 7,500 buses covering the length and breadth of Britain.

The law of unintended consequences came in to play in the British bus manufacturing industry. First, the government's support for operators with the new bus grant in the 1970s had fuelled sales of new buses, and when the grant was phased out in the early 1980s there was a slow-down in orders. Second, while local bus deregulation had

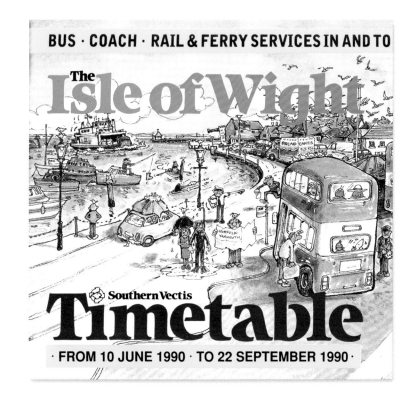

BUS · COACH · RAIL & FERRY SERVICES IN AND TO

The Isle of Wight

Southern Vectis **Timetable**

· FROM 10 JUNE 1990 · TO 22 SEPTEMBER 1990 ·

➤ Whilst the style of presentation of NBC bus timetables may have varied, once they became independent some former NBC subsidiaries were eager to adopt a new and more adventurous approach to cover design. This colourful timetable cover was commissioned by Southern Vectis in 1990 from local cartoonist Rupert Besley.

re-invigorated the bus industry, most operators investing in new vehicles in the mid-1980s were buying minibuses, and this had a significant impact on the manufacturers of traditional full-size buses. And third, privatisation coming on top of deregulation added to the climate of uncertainty, further reducing investment in new buses.

Leyland was affected badly: the bigger they come, the harder they fall. It closed four bus factories in the 1980s – Park Royal (1980), Bristol (1983), Roe (1984) and ECW (1987). Roe would enjoy a new and occasionally turbulent lease of life as Optare, but the others simply disappeared. Outside the Leyland group, other established businesses which shut down were MCW (1989) and Duple (1990). Northern Counties called in the administrators in 1991 but survived as a going concern.

Minibus mania created a short-lived boom for a few coachbuilders who then faded from the scene, such as Carlyle, Dormobile, Reeve Burgess (absorbed by parent company Plaxton), Robin Hood and PMT.

It wasn't all bad news. Dennis was making some headway with the Dominator double-decker which it had launched in 1977, and the company grew rapidly from the late 1980s with its Dart midibus and Javelin coach chassis. And it was Dennis which led the move to cost-effective low-floor buses with the introduction of the Lance SLF in 1993, followed by the Dart SLF in 1995.

Mainland European manufacturers benefited from the retrenchment in British bus manufacturing, with DAF, Scania and

POINTER

REEVE BURGESS

Volvo winning more business from both coach and bus operators. Volvo further secured its already strong position in Britain when it purchased Leyland Bus in 1988.

It is hard to over-emphasise the extent of the transformation that was seen in the British bus industry between 1980 and 2000. NBC, SBG, the PTEs and most municipal operators vanished. In their place there were new British groups, some with operations in other parts of the world. Subsidiaries of Stagecoach, First, Arriva and Go-Ahead now provided a significant percentage of Britain's bus services, while just a handful of companies survived as recognisable successors to pre-deregulation NBC businesses – most notably East Yorkshire, Southern Vectis, Trent, Wilts & Dorset and Yorkshire Traction.

But all of these except Trent and East Yorkshire would go on to be acquired by larger groups in the early years of the new century, and East Yorkshire would eventually be bought by Go-Ahead in 2018.

The changes were more subtle in London, where the regulatory regime differed from that in the rest of Britain. In 2000 London's buses were still mainly red, but instead of being operated by a single entity most services were run under contract by eleven British private sector companies, one Singapore-based transport business and a state-financed French conglomerate.

These were two momentous and tumultuous decades, arguably unparalleled in the history of Britain's bus industry. ■

3
No longer National – the end of NBC

Northern General abandoned NBC's poppy red in favour of a darker shade applied in traditional style. This Roe-bodied Leyland Atlantean, one of 40 delivered in 1980, has just crossed the River Wear as it approaches Sunderland town centre in 1986. It retains the standard NBC-style fleetname, but prefixed by 'Go-Ahead'.

187 Sunderland

NORTHERN

AUP 372W

I n 1969, with a fleet of 20,637 buses and coaches, the state-owned National Bus Company claimed to be the world's biggest bus operator. In 1980 the fleet stood at 15,538, a reduction of 25 per cent in just eleven years, but still an impressive figure.

To take an analogy from 20 years later, NBC had grown into something akin to the emerging commercial bus groups of the 1990s all rolled into one, plus a lot more besides. But a big difference was that unlike those groups, in most urban areas NBC was not the predominant operator. Instead, its fleets augmented the urban services of local authority operators across England and Wales, sometimes working in coordination with them, and its activities extended to outlying areas and between population centres.

That being said, through various historical vagaries NBC did have the role of major bus service provider in a number of substantial towns and cities including Bristol, Carlisle, Gloucester, Norwich, Stoke-on-Trent, Swansea and York.

Another difference was that NBC had retained more clearly recognisable regional subsidiary companies than the groups that eventually succeeded it, each with its own familiar fleetname and management structure. However, by 1980 the differentiation was quite limited visually, since NBC had adopted a corporate identity in 1972.

▲ The Tilling group was one of the major constituents of the National Bus Company and it had a conservative vehicle policy, not switching from front-engined Bristol Lodekkas to rear-engined VRTs until 1969. The legacy of this policy was that some 500 Lodekkas were still in NBC service in 1980. The biggest fleet was operated by Bristol Omnibus, which had around 100. This smart 1965 bus was a late survivor, seen here in central Bristol in the summer of 1983.

▼ Designed jointly by Leyland and NBC, the Leyland National was, unsurprisingly, the most numerous type of single-decker in NBC service at the start of the 1980s. This is a late example of the original model with the Leyland 500-series engine. It entered service with United Counties in December 1979 at the same time as the first of the 680-powered National 2s were being delivered to other NBC subsidiaries. This is Milton Keynes in 1981; the barely-discernible Milton Keynes Citybus branding behind the rear wheel is eclipsed by the advert for East Midlands Electricity.

Most of the familiar fleetnames were retained, but out went the long-established liveries of NBC's operating companies, replaced by either poppy red or leaf green which, even by the unexacting standards of the time, was spectacularly uninspiring. Writing in *The History of British Bus Services* in 1989, transport historian John Hibbs observed that "a single house style in so individualistic an industry is a lowest common denominator of dullness." Few would argue with that.

But at the start of the 1980s change was in the air. It began early in the period as some of NBC's constituent companies were reorganised, the biggest of them being divided into smaller units. The first change came in 1981, involving Midland Red. The company's core urban business had been sold to the West Midlands PTE in 1973, leaving it with a fleet of around 850 vehicles and a ring of services in the counties surrounding the PTE area. These were now shared between four new companies with the points of the compass as part of their name in the style Midland Red West. A fifth company, Midland Express, took over the coach operations.

There were major changes in south-west England in 1983 affecting Bristol Omnibus, Western National and Hants & Dorset.

Two new companies, Cheltenham & Gloucester and Swindon & District, took over Bristol's operations in these areas. The were further changes in 1986 when Bristol's remaining country services passed to a new company imaginatively named Badgerline.

Western National's territory was reduced to Cornwall. The remainder of its business was taken over by three new companies based in Exeter, Taunton and Barnstaple. The first two revived old names, Devon General and Southern National; the third was North Devon.

The reorganisation of Hants & Dorset saw the revival of three old names, Wilts & Dorset, Provincial and Shamrock & Rambler. The first two were bus operators, while Shamrock & Rambler operated coaches from bases in Bournemouth and Southampton. After less

◄ Imaginative marketing by Devon General in 1986 saw Humphrey Bogart and Ingrid Bergman (or at least a suggestion of her) enlisted to promote minibus services in Exeter. The song *As Time Goes By* was featured in the 1942 film *Casablanca*, starring Bogart and Bergman.

▲ The National 2 was immediately identifiable by its revised front end, necessary to accommodate the radiator, which had been relocated from the rear of the bus to the front to make space for the bigger 680 engine. This bus was new in 1980 to Bristol Omnibus and was later operated by Cheltenham & Gloucester, a company created in 1983 to take over Bristol's northern operations. Cheltenham area buses (and those in Swindon) adopted NBC poppy red, as seen here in Gloucester bus station – a break with Bristol's NBC leaf green, but scarcely revolutionary at a time when bigger changes were in the air. This photograph was taken in 1988 after privatisation; the NBC logo which sat to the left of the Cheltenham District fleetname has been removed.

▼ The Gloucester operations of Cheltenham & Gloucester adopted a blue livery with City of Gloucester fleetnames. Although the colours were still applied in NBC proportions, the strong shade of blue gave the fleet a crisp new look. Only the logos identify this 1975 Bristol VRT seen in Gloucester in 1984 as an NBC bus. It was one of four that Cheltenham & Gloucester acquired from United Auto in 1983.

NBC vehicle policy

In the early 1980s NBC companies largely maintained their existing vehicle purchasing policies. Most of the double-deck buses delivered to the organisation in the 1970s had been ECW-bodied Bristol VRTs, backed up by over 600 Leyland Atlantean AN68s with bodies by Park Royal and Roe, both to the same design, and also by Eastern Coach Works, in this case to a design similar to that used for full-height Bristol VRTs. There were also 57 VRTs with unusual full-height Willowbrook bodies. Single-deck buses were mainly Leyland Nationals or Bristol LHs.

In December 1979 production at the Leyland National factory in Workington switched from the original model with Leyland's 500-series engine to a revised model, the National 2, with the 680 engine as used in the Leopard coach chassis. At the same time the smaller Bristol LH chassis, typically used by NBC as a rural bus, was being phased out of production. The last of these for NBC – short LHS models – entered service with National Welsh in 1981.

There were double-deck changes, too. The last Bristol VRTs – of which there were almost 3,700 in NBC service – were delivered in 1981 alongside the first of the replacement model, the Leyland Olympian, which initially was built at the Bristol factory.

NBC's last Atlanteans also entered service in 1981, and from then on the Olympian ruled... well, almost. In 1980 NBC bought 25 MCW Metrobuses. Then in 1982 it severed its financial ties with Leyland, which dated back to a 1965 arrangement under which Leyland had acquired an interest in Bristol Commercial Vehicles and Eastern Coach Works.

This development removed some of NBC's incentive to buy Leyland group products, and indeed it added a further 108 Metrobuses between 1983 and 1986. However, to put that in perspective, by 1986 it had purchased just over 1,000 Olympians.

NBC's coach operations had since 1972 used a white livery. Most of the coaches were Leyland Leopards, typically with Plaxton or Duple bodies. The deregulation of coach services in 1980 saw new operators challenging NBC on many of its trunk routes. However NBC responded quickly with high-specification coaches, most of which from 1982 were Leyland Tigers. To increase capacity on its busiest routes NBC bought double-deck MCW Metroliners, able to seat up to 71 passengers on coaches fitted with toilets. Their reliability proved suspect, though their imposing design certainly cut a dash on the road. NBC also bought long-wheelbase Olympian coaches for London commuter routes operated by Alder Valley, Eastern National, London Country and Maidstone & District.

In its bus operations, the big change at NBC was the switch to small vehicles. Between 1984 and 1986, in the face of the competition that was expected to arise from impending deregulation, NBC bought some 4,000 minibuses based mainly on Ford Transit, Freight Rover Sherpa and Iveco Daily chassis and Mercedes-Benz L608D vans. Purchases of full-size buses slowed right down. The small buses were promoted with enthusiasm, bright liveries and catchy names. It was all a far cry from the uniformity of NBC's corporate identity.

◄ Another new NBC subsidiary to adopt a blue livery was Cambus, created in 1984 to take over the Cambridgeshire operations of Eastern Counties. This 1969 VRT with the original flat-front style of ECW body was the oldest of 64 VRTs that Cambus acquired from Eastern Counties. This is a 1985 view. In some lights the pale Cambus fleetname was was barely visible against the somewhat pallid blue of the livery.

◄ What were described as local coaches in NBC parlance carried this style of livery in the 1970s, with red or green lower panels and white for the window surrounds and roof. More imaginative schemes would appear in the 1980s. This 49-seat Willowbrook-bodied Leyland Leopard in the Maidstone & District fleet had been new in 1968. It waits in Maidstone High Street in 1980 for passengers for Bearsted.

NBC privatisation

Company	Fleet	Sold	Buyer
Alder Valley South	226	1987	Frontsource
Ambassador Travel	40	1987	Management
Badgerline	400	1986	Management/employees
Berks Bucks Bus Co	180	1987	Q Drive
Brighton & Hove	220	1987	Management
Bristol Omnibus	394	1987	Midland Red West/management
Cambus	269	1986	Management
Cheltenham & Gloucester	200	1986	Management (Western Travel)
City of Oxford	157	1987	Management
Crosville	470	1988	ATL
Crosville Wales	470	1987	Management
Cumberland	230	1987	Stagecoach
Devon General	400	1986	Management
East Kent	320	1987	Management
East Midland	260	1988	Management
East Yorkshire	300	1987	Management
Eastern Counties	340	1987	Management
Eastern National	526	1986	Management
Green Line Travel	-	-	(a)
Hastings & District	100	1987	Management
Hampshire Bus/Pilgrim Coaches	243	1987	Stagecoach
Kentish Bus & Coach	168	1988	Proudmutual
Lincolnshire	172	1988	Yorkshire Traction
London Country North East	316	1988	Alan Stephenson/Parkdale Holdings
London Country North West	360	1988	Management
London Country South West	415	1988	Drawlane
Luton & District	260	1987	Employees
Maidstone & District	300	1986	Management
Midland Fox	353	1987	Management (b)
Midland Red North	248	1988	Drawlane
Midland Red South	180	1987	Western Travel
Midland Red West and Midland Red Coaches	382	1986	Management
Milton Keynes City Bus	144	1987	Management
National Express	4	1988	Management
National Holidays	-	1986	Pleasurama
National Travel East	84	1987	ATL
National Travelworld	-	1988	Badgerline
National Welsh	410	1987	Management
North Western	340	1988	Drawlane
Northern General	730	1987	Management
Northumbria	319	1987	Management (Proudmutual)

Company	Fleet	Sold	Buyer
PMT	300	1986	Management
Provincial	90	1987	Employees
Ribble	700	1988	Management
Shamrock & Rambler	73	1987	Drawlane
South Midland	110	1986	Management
South Wales	265	1987	Management
Southdown	320	1987	Management
Southern National and North Devon	300	1988	Management
Southern Vectis	130	1986	Management
Trent	350	1986	Management
United Automobile	490	1987	Caldaire
United Counties	250	1987	Stagecoach
Victoria Coach Station	-	1988	London Regional Transport
Voyage National	6	1987	Eastern National
Wessex National	43	1987	Management
West Riding/Yorkshire Woollen	425	1987	Management (Caldaire)
West Yorkshire	400	1987	Alan Stephenson/management/Parkdale
Western National	300	1987	Plympton Coachlines/Badgerline
Wilts & Dorset	210	1987	Management
Yorkshire Traction	361	1987	Management

(a) Ownership of Green Line Travel was shared between the four former London Country businesses.

(b) Stevensons of Uttoxeter took over the Swadlincote depot of Midland Fox, with 44 vehicles.

● Alan Stephenson, involved in the London Country North East and West Yorkshire purchases, was chairman of East Yorkshire Motor Services.

● Pleasurama was the owner of holiday coach tour operator Smiths-Shearings.

All NBC's engineering companies were bought by Frontsource in 1987–88:

Alder Valley Engineering
Bristol Engineering
Carlyle Works
Eastern National Engineering
Gatwick Engineering
H&D Distribution
Kent Engineering
Southdown Engineering
United Counties Engineering

◄ Where a smaller bus than a Leyland National was needed, NBC's preferred choice was the Bristol LH6L with Leyland 400-series engine and 43-seat ECW body. This was one of the last, new to Bristol Omnibus in 1980 but operating with Wilts & Dorset in Bournemouth when photographed in 1985. The lower front panel has been modified to improve the approach angle on routes which used the Sandbanks Ferry across Poole Harbour.

▼ NBC's standard double-decker in the 1980s was the Leyland Olympian with ECW body, typically with 77 seats. An East Midland example, new in 1984, loads in Chesterfield in the summer of 1985. Like most NBC Olympians, and most VRTs before them, it had a Gardner engine.

▲ Variations on this striped livery were adopted by a number of NBC subsidiaries, primarily for coaches on short-distance express services which were not part of the National Express network. In a break with tradition City of Oxford used blue and yellow for the City Link service to London, as illustrated on a 1977 Leyland Leopard with Duple Dominant body which had been new to PMT. The coach is pulling out of Victoria Coach Station in the summer of 1984.

than nine months as a stand-alone business Shamrock & Rambler's Southampton fleet was set up as a separate company, Pilgrim Coaches, at the start of 1984. The Hants & Dorset name disappeared as the company's Hampshire operations were taken over by a new Hampshire Bus company.

There were two smaller splits in 1983. City of Oxford's South Midland fleet was established as a separate business, while the Hastings operations of Maidstone & District were formed as a new Hastings & District company.

Eastern Counties was divided in 1984, when its operations in and around Cambridgeshire were taken over by new company, Cambus, leaving a smaller Eastern Counties company serving Norfolk and Suffolk. Eastern Counties' coaching business passed to another new company, Ambassador Travel.

The biggest changes came at the start of 1986, just ahead of deregulation and privatisation. United Counties was united no longer. Its fleet was halved from 500 to 250 buses. The rest of the business was divided between two new companies, Luton & District (187 buses) and Milton Keynes Citybus (64). On the south coast, Southdown lost its urban services in and around Brighton. These were taken over by the newly created Brighton & Hove Bus and Coach Co, echoing the name of a company which had been combined with Southdown in the early days of NBC. And Alder Valley was split in two, Alder Valley South, based in Guildford, and Alder Valley North with its headquarters in Bracknell. In 1987 Alder Valley North changed its name to the Berks Bucks Bus Company, trading as The Bee Line in a yellow livery.

Later in 1986 Ribble was reduced in size. Its services in Penrith and Carlisle were transferred to Cumberland Motor Services (a rare instance of a change involving two existing companies), and its operations in Wigan and Merseyside were taken over by a new North Western company. Crosville was split in two, with the new Crosville Wales taking over the Welsh depots. In the north-east of England

◄ London Country Bus Services' first big order for double-deckers called for 90 Leyland Atlantean PDR1As with 72-seat dual-door Park Royal bodies. They were delivered in 1972; this one is seen in Guildford in 1984. Further similar buses would follow until 1981, but on the improved AN68 Atlantean chassis and of single-door layout. From 1979 the bodies were supplied by Roe following the closure of Park Royal.

▼ In 1980 the South Yorkshire PTE withdrew 18 Bristol VRTs which had been new to Sheffield Transport in 1972 and were non-standard in the PTE fleet. All were bought by NBC, with 12 going to Maidstone & District and six to Crosville. In 1983 M&D's operations in Hastings were taken over by a new Hastings & District company, which adopted a distinctive maroon livery as seen in 1984 on one of the ex-South Yorkshire VRTs. The body was by East Lancs.

United Auto saw the new Northumbria Motor Services take on its operations in Northumberland, while its services in Scarborough passed to the long-established East Yorkshire Motor Services, which adopted Scarborough & District as the name for the former United operations. United survived as a mere shadow of its former self.

Finally, the biggest of NBC's subsidiaries, London Country Bus Services with just over 1,200 buses and coaches, was divided into four segments around London, named in the style of London Country North West, North East, South East and South West. London Country South East was the first to break completely with tradition, abandoning the green livery long associated with London's country buses and replacing it with a bright cream and maroon. At the same time the business was renamed the Kentish Bus & Coach Company.

The net result of all these reorganisations was that the number of bus and coach operating subsidiaries of NBC rose from 35 in 1980 to 59 when the privatisation process got under way in 1986.

The various splits in existing NBC companies certainly brought a distinct visual change; the corporate look was gradually replaced by a range of new identities. It is easy to forget in hindsight that this started to happen while the companies were still in NBC ownership, reflecting a radical shift in policy from the years of rigid uniformity. Admittedly, the initial changes were tentative – white added to Northern General's red, a new shade of red at Midland Red East – but gradually confidence grew. A strong blue scheme was introduced at Gloucester, for instance, though still in NBC's simple layout.

But soon there were much bolder moves, as many companies got rid of the corporate NBC look altogether. For example, Northumbria and North Western adopted distinctive liveries with diagonal colour breaks. Badgerline adopted a bright yellow and green, and Bristol a jaunty red, yellow and blue. Midland Fox, the new name for Midland Red East, added a yellow front to its darker red livery. Southdown reverted to apple green and cream, the company's traditional colours.

NBC's businesses were privatised between July 1986 and April 1988, as summarised in the table on page 16. Most of the bus-operating subsidiaries were bought by their managers and most

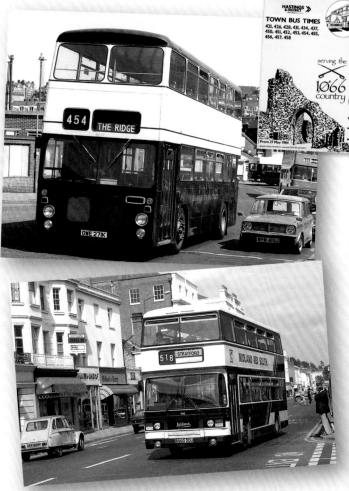

▲ A few NBC subsidiaries specified high-backed seats in ECW-bodied Olympians, primarily for use on interurban services. Two joined the Midland Red South fleet in 1984 and had 70 seats, which compared with 77 on standard bus-seated Olympians delivered at the same time. This one, in a two-tone red and white adaptation of NBC's striped local coach livery, is leaving Leamington Spa for Stratford-upon-Avon in the summer of 1985.

◄ South Midland, split from City of Oxford Motor Services in 1983, adopted a maroon and cream livery, echoing colours used by the company in pre-NBC days. This Bristol VRT had been new to City of Oxford in 1975 and is seen in the city in the spring of 1986; South Midland, one of NBC's smallest subsidiaries with 110 vehicles, was bought by its management at the end of that year.

◄ Six NBC Olympian coaches received this style of ECW body, which used the standard bus frame, but with a stylish new front and with fixed side windows. Alder Valley North took three in 1986 for its Londonlink services. The other three, on long-wheelbase chassis, went to Eastern National.

▼ The second-hand bus market was flooded with ex-Greater Manchester PTE buses in 1986–87. Many were bought by the new breed of independents taking advantage of deregulation to launch bus services. But a few found their way into major fleets, as illustrated by a Northern Counties-bodied Daimler Fleetline operating a local service in Leamington Spa in the spring of 1988, soon after joining the Midland Red South fleet. The company had been bought by Western Travel in December 1987, and the Fleetline has been repainted in corporate NBC style but without the NBC logo.

buy-outs proved to be successful. Many of the resultant businesses, most notably Badgerline, would go on to acquire other former NBC companies in the late 1980s and early 1990s.

The biggest failure was National Welsh, a company created by NBC in 1978 to take over Red & White and Western Welsh, then running 700 vehicles. In 1987 it was the second-biggest bus company in Wales, now with 410 vehicles. In 1988–89 it took over the services of three struggling municipal companies in the South Wales valleys, an area which proved a hotbed of competitive activity. That National Welsh bought 250 minibuses between 1986 and 1989 gives some idea of the frenetic activity in its area. But the tide quickly turned. In 1991 its eastern operations, which traded as Red & White with 180 vehicles, were bought by Western Travel. In 1992 the remainder of the business closed, after parts of it were sold to other operators, including a consortium trading as Rhondda Buses. ∎

▲ Most NBC coaches were bodied by the two mainstream British builders, Duple and Plaxton. But in 1981–82 the main order for coach bodies was placed with ECW, which provided 155 bodies on Leyland Leopard and Tiger chassis. The end result could best be described as workmanlike. The structure was based on that used for bodies on Bristol RE coaches built ten years earlier. On the mid-engined Leylands there was insufficient support for the rear luggage compartment, a problem which only manifested itself after the first coaches entered service. Although carrying National Holidays branding, this 1982 Leopard in the Southern Vectis fleet is operating on a National Express service.

▼ A striking contrast to the basic ECW-bodied Leopard is provided by this 71-seat Plaxton Paramount 4000, one of five supplied to Yorkshire Traction in 1986. It had a Neoplan underframe and a 320bhp Gardner 15.5-litre 6LYT engine. NBC bought 28 Neoplan-based Paramount 4000s.

Unhappy with buses supplied by Leyland, Irish transport operator CIE teamed up with two North American businesses, Bombardier and GAC, to build a range of bespoke buses in Ireland. These included a light-weight country bus, and one of these with a Cummins engine was supplied to NBC as a demonstrator at the start of 1986 and allocated to United Auto. This photograph was taken during a press demonstration in February; before entering service the bus was repainted white with overall advertising for Cummins, which had a factory in Darlington. It was bought by Bus Eireann in early 1988.

Between 1968 and 1981 NBC and its Tilling Group predecessor bought 3,669 new Bristol VRTs, all but 57 with ECW bodies. Most were standard lowheight models, 13ft 8in high, as illustrated by the bus on the right. The other most common variant was the full-height, 14ft 6in, model, specified by a small number of operators and seen on the left. The third variant is illustrated by the bus in the centre, which is just 13ft 5in high. This body could most easily be identified by the absence of the band of white relief above the windscreen. All three buses were new to Maidstone & District but are seen here at Hastings railway station in 1984 in the ownership of the recently-formed Hastings & District company.

▼ PMT was another company to adopt a new livery while still part of NBC – note the logo below the windscreen. This is a 1979 VRT, in Newcastle-under-Lyme in May 1986. The company was bought by its management at the end of the year.

▼ After Crosville was divided into separate English and Welsh companies in 1986 the one based in England adopted this unusual orange and green livery – an emphatic break from the uniform green used by NBC, then still its parent. It is shown on a 1979 Bristol VRT in Manchester. This livery was short-lived; the orange was soon replaced by cream.

◄ Like Northern General, Midland Red West adopted a new livery which reflected the company's heritage. This is one of 20 Marshall-bodied Leyland Leopards delivered to the original Midland Red company in 1974, passing to Midland Red West in 1981 and seen in Kidderminster in 1987, shortly after the business had been privatised in a management buy-out. It was withdrawn in 1990.

Hampshire Bus adopted this distinctive livery, seen on an example of that ubiquitous NBC model, the Bristol VRT. It was new in 1975 to Hants & Dorset, and is pulling out of Winchester bus station in May 1987, a few weeks after the company had been bought by Stagecoach.

➤ Not all minibuses were on urban services. A Freight Rover Sherpa was an appropriate choice for the Snowdon Sherpa which had been introduced by Crosville in 1976 as a park-and-ride service for hikers and climbers. In 1987 it was being run by Crosville Wales as part of a network funded by Gwynedd council. Gwynedd required that buses used on council-supported routes have a red front with Bws Gwynedd branding.

⋀ By the time the revised Leyland National 2 was introduced at the end of 1979 NBC's interest in big single-deck buses was beginning to wane. In 1985, the last year of National production, NBC took delivery of just ten, eight of which were for Southdown. One is seen in the ownership of Brighton & Hove in 1987, exiting a bus lane designed to reduce delays to buses approaching central Brighton from the north.

➤ In 1988 National Welsh added green to its original NBC red and white livery, paying homage to the colour combination found on the Welsh flag. A 1978 VRT illustrates the point. It is leaving Cardiff bus station in 1989 and would be withdrawn the following year. National Welsh itself had a short future. It closed in 1992.

➤ This full-page advert appeared in transport trade magazines when the privatisation of NBC was getting under way.

▼ Provincial was an employee buy-out from NBC and its new owners adopted People's Provincial as its trading name, with a livery which reflected that used by the pre-NBC Provincial business. This Leyland National had been new to Red & White in 1975. It was one of a number purchased from National Welsh in 1987 and is seen in Portsmouth in 1989, showing that with proper attention 14-year-old buses can look smart. The red wheels were a nice touch.

SEVENTY GREAT NAMES FOR SALE

NATIONAL BUS COMPANY IS BEING PRIVATISED

The State-owned National Bus Company is being privatised — not as one company, not in regional groups, but as around 70 individual companies. Companies with well-known local names like Southdown, Crosville, Midland Red and Yorkshire Traction.

The companies for sale include bus and coach companies, engineering companies and the nationally-known names, National Express and National Travelworld, the travel agency chain.

And the sale is now on.

Many companies have a long tradition and are closely involved with their local communities.

The privatisation of National Bus provides opportunities for purchasers to become involved in progressive transport and leisure travel businesses.

Here are some of the options:

1. You can make an offer for a bus or coach company.

2. You could consider a joint venture with the local management team.

3. You could obtain a valuable advertising medium through involvement with a bus company.

If you would like further information, please contact the Chairman, National Bus Company, 172 Buckingham Palace Road, London SW1W 9TN.

DENNIS DOMINO

The Dennis Domino was developed to meet the Greater Manchester PTE's need for a small bus to replace a fleet of Seddon Pennines operating on the Centreline service in Manchester. This connected Piccadilly and Victoria railway stations with the main shopping and business areas. The Seddons, developed in the early 1970s, were OK – but no more than that. The Pennine (illustrated on page 31) had a noisy front-mounted engine, a narrow entrance and a high floor.

The Domino offered a wider entrance and a lower floor and the engine, a 5.8-litre Perkins 6.354, was mounted at the rear. At 25ft (7.6m) long and 7ft 6in (2.3m) wide the Domino anticipated a much more successful midibus – the Dennis Dart.

Just 34 Dominos were built, 20 for Greater Manchester and 14 for the South Yorkshire PTE. All entered service towards the end of 1985. The Domino was over-engineered and heavy. Those running in Manchester weighed almost 6.8 tonnes, which was around one tonne heavier than the Dennis Darts being built four years later.

▼ The South Yorkshire PTE chose Optare to body its Dominos. This is Fitzalan Square in Sheffield in 1990. When new the buses carried a less colourful livery with Nipper, rather than Little Nipper, as the fleetname.

▲ Northern Counties produced an attractive body for the Greater Manchester PTE's Dominos. The Centreline fare in 1986 was 15p. The prominent phone number on the front is part of an advert for British Rail's Red Star parcel deliveries.

4
Chaos out of order for the PTEs

With Liverpool's imposing river-front buildings in the background, a typical Merseyside PTE Alexander-bodied Leyland Atlantean leaves the bus station at the Woodside ferry terminal in Birkenhead. This is a 1988 view, when the bus was owned by the PTE's arm's-length company, Merseyside Transport, which traded as Merseybus. The Atlantean was new in 1974 but is representative of almost 550 broadly similar buses purchased by the PTE between 1972 and 1984.

In 1980 passenger transport executives provided bus services in seven major urban areas in Britain outside London. The aim of the Labour government which had set them up was to provide an improved co-ordinated transport network, akin to that which operated in London. The PTEs were established between 1969 and 1974 and took over the bus operations of 33 municipal transport departments and almost 11,000 buses in the West Midlands, South Yorkshire, West Yorkshire, Greater Manchester (known as South East Lancashire and North East Cheshire until re-formed in 1974), Merseyside, Tyneside (later Tyne & Wear) and Greater Glasgow.

The municipal fleets that were acquired by the new undertakings ranged in size from Birmingham City Transport, which had 1,400 buses, to Ramsbottom Urban District Council with 12, and the number of council fleets absorbed ranged from eleven in Greater Manchester to just one in Glasgow.

Although London was the model for the PTEs, unlike the original London Passenger Transport Board of the 1930s they had no powers of compulsory purchase over bus operators in their areas. Two, Selnec and West Midlands, reached agreements with the National Bus Company to buy some of its local bus operations. In Tyne & Wear and West Yorkshire the local NBC operators painted some of their buses in PTE livery, or an approximation of it. NBC buses in Merseyside carried the PTE logo alongside the company fleetname.

In 1980 the PTEs owned just under 10,500 buses. In descending order of size these were owned by:

Greater Manchester	2,878
West Midlands	2,499
West Yorkshire	1,323
Merseyside	1,235
South Yorkshire	1,024
Greater Glasgow	973
Tyne & Wear	547

▲ With delays to deliveries of the West Midlands PTE's preferred chassis, the Fleetline, an order was placed for 50 Volvo Ailsas with Alexander bodies. They were delivered in 1976. All were sold to London Buses in 1987. This example is seen heading north out of central Birmingham through a brutalist concrete cityscape that has changed out of all recognition since the picture was taken in the spring of 1983.

▼ Bradford Corporation was the original owner of this Leyland Atlantean, a relatively unusual long-wheelbase PDR2/1 model. It was part of an order for 70 outwardly-similar Alexander-bodied buses comprising 40 Daimler Fleetlines and 30 Atlanteans, delivered in 1970–71. Bradford was one of the constituents of the West Yorkshire PTE, in whose ownership the bus is seen in 1983 passing the 1977 Bradford Interchange, a bold PTE project which combined bus and train stations, plus a garage to house all the PTE's Bradford-based buses.

◄ In 1979 the Tyne & Wear PTE took delivery of 90 new buses with this style of MCW body, comprising 40 Fleetlines and 50 Atlanteans. An Atlantean joins Northumberland Street, Newcastle's prime shopping street, heading north from the city centre towards Kenton Bar. The name refers to a former toll bar and later a pub of the same name at the west end of Kenton Lane. It is now known chiefly for its 1960s housing estate.

◄ NBC's Northern General subsidiary adopted a yellow livery for local buses in the Tyne & Wear PTE area. Initially it was applied in standard NBC style, as seen on a brand-new Roe-bodied Atlantean in the Northern fleet in 1980. Later cream was used in place of the white relief, and eventually both Northern and United Auto adopted the PTE's full livery for operations in its area.

The PTEs had been established to improve bus services through coordination. That changed in 1986 when the Conservative government of the time decided that the way to improve bus services was not through coordination, but through competition. The PTEs were instructed to establish limited companies to take over their bus operations, which were to be run commercially. However the PTEs retained some oversight of bus operations, most visibly in the awarding of tenders to provide socially-desirable services which had not been registered commercially by any operator.

In most PTE areas the competition was intense in the early years of deregulation, usually from a myriad of small operators running elderly second-hand vehicles.

In Glasgow the competition facing the PTE's Strathclyde Buses business was particularly fierce. The Scottish Bus Group's 1985 reorganisation had created two new companies, Clydeside and Kelvin, to serve the Greater Glasgow area. Part of their deregulation strategy was to launch new high-frequency cross-city services with around 100 redundant London Routemasters. Stagecoach, too,

appeared in Glasgow with Routemasters. The good citizens of Glasgow had never seen so many buses.

The Tyne & Wear PTE's bus company was named Busways Travel Services. It operated through three main divisions – Newcastle, South Shields and Sunderland – supported by low-cost units trading under brands such as Blue Bus and Economic. One of its major competitors was the Tyne & Wear Omnibus Company, set up by long-standing independent Trimdon Motor Services. Tyne & Wear Omnibus built up a fleet of around 100 mostly elderly single-decker buses, but was bought by Busways in 1989.

Greater Manchester was probably the region hit hardest by deregulation. The PTE's company was GM Buses, and at the outset its fleet was reduced by some 450 buses from its pre-deregulation level. And it was facing much more than the large number of small operators that typically had appeared in other conurbations. United Transport, a British company with substantial bus operations in Africa, launched new services in Manchester and Stockport in 1987 with 225 minibuses branded as The Bee Line

◄ The Mancunian, developed by Manchester City Transport, was the first British double-decker designed specifically for one-person operation. With its squared-off styling and deep windscreens it was a turning point in the design of double-deck buses. Translucent roof panels made the upper saloon brighter. This Mancunian running for the Greater Manchester PTE in 1981 has a long-wheelbase Leyland Atlantean chassis and an East Lancs body. It was new in 1970.

◄ As well as investing in vehicles, the Greater Manchester PTE made a significant investment in bus stations. This is Rochdale, opened in 1978. In the foreground is a PTE standard Leyland Fleetline with Northern Counties body, with a Leyland National and another standard double-decker, in this case an Atlantean, behind. The PTE's buses generally did not carry their manufacturers' badges so to differentiate between standard Atlanteans and Fleetlines enthusiasts had to rely on fleet numbers or identification features such as the style of the engine cover.

▲ Working with Seddon, the Selnec PTE developed a midibus in 1972 at a time when such vehicles were rare. The idea was continued by Greater Manchester, and at the start of the 1980s a fleet of these compact buses was running the Centreline service which connected the main railway stations with the central shopping and business areas. The flat fare in 1980 was 10p, advertised on the slip board below the windscreen. The buses had four-cylinder Perkins engines and Seddon bodies and buzzed around the city until being replaced by Dennis Dominos in 1985.

▲ Four of Manchester's Seddon midis were purchased by the Greater Glasgow PTE in 1978 and were operated until 1987. This is one of the original 1972 models, with a different style of Seddon body from the later buses, as shown left. It is leaving Glasgow Central station in the summer of 1982 for the short hop to the city's other terminal station, in Queen Street. In Glasgow the sign under the windscreen advises, "Exact fare. No change given," but rather unhelpfully neglects to say what the fare is.

Buzz company. GM Buses responded by expanding its fleet of Little Gem minibuses.

Merseybus, the PTE company serving Liverpool and its surroundings, faced competition from Crosville and North Western, as well as various new operators, some of which were started by redundant PTE employees. A few of these even used redundant PTE buses to compete with their former employer. Prominent newcomers in Liverpool were Fareway (1986), Liver Line (1988) and Liverbus (1990).

Yorkshire Rider was the West Yorkshire PTE's bus company. As in the other PTE areas, there was competition in the main centres of population. The biggest threat, which never materialised, came from United Transport which planned a minibus operation in Leeds, similar to those it had launched in Manchester and Preston. To dissuade United from starting new services Yorkshire Rider introduced 120 minibuses to its fleet in 1987. Most were Freight Rover Sherpas, which were promoted under the Micro Rider brand.

The main competition for South Yorkshire Transport, as that PTE's bus company was known, appeared in Sheffield. Most of it came from small companies but Caldaire, the 1987 buy-out of NBC's West Riding and Yorkshire Woollen business, set up Sheffield & District with a fleet which grew to include 14 brand-new Leyland Lynxes. SYT's response to its competitors included introducing Eager Beaver minibus services and the introduction of the Mainline brand, initially

▲ The Greater Glasgow PTE was renamed Strathclyde in 1980, and between 1980 and 1983 used this unusual livery with Trans-Clyde fleetnames. A 1983 MCW Metrobus II heads through the city centre in 1984 passing the Boots clock, for many years a city landmark and meeting point.

▼ The Strathclyde PTE favoured Ailsas, most of which had Alexander R-type bodies, and by 1984 had built up a fleet of 152. This bus was new in 1982. Because the Ailsa's engine was at the front, between the driving position and the passenger doorway, the driver had to enter the cab by an external offside door, as he or she would have done on traditional half-cab models.

➤ Among the more unusual examples of diversification by PTEs was the introduction of services to London from Birmingham by the West Midlands PTE and from Newcastle upon Tyne by Tyne & Wear. The latter used MCW Metroliners operated by its Armstrong-Galley fleet, created in 1973 with the acquisition of two independent coach operators. The blue livery was inspired by a Scania demonstrator. Most Metroliners were purchased by NBC; relatively few found their way into other operators' fleets. Tyne & Wear had six. This one was new in 1984 and had 69 seats plus a toilet.

◄ The South Yorkshire PTE used this uninspiring livery, here on a 1976 Roe-bodied Fleetline in Rotherham. Where there was a measure of body standardisation in most of the other PTEs in the 1970s, South Yorkshire sourced bodywork from most of Britain's bodybuilders including Alexander, East Lancs, ECW and MCW, as well as Roe.

➤ Greater Manchester Buses, the PTE's deregulation-era bus company, introduced new coaches and a new livery for selected limited-stop services, including the Trans-Lancs Express. This coach in Stockport, nearing the end of its journey from Bolton, was the first of 30 Northern Counties-bodied MCW Metrobuses, a combination unique to GM Buses. It was photographed in September 1986 when just a few weeks old.

for a busy Sheffield cross-city service but eventually adopted across the fleet.

West Midlands Travel was perhaps the most successful of the PTE companies in terms of protecting its core network. Like all the others it faced competition from new operators on a number of fronts, but it registered the equivalent of 81 per cent of its service network, compared with around 70 per cent by most of the other English PTEs' new bus companies.

One little-remarked victim of deregulation was the 600m-long guided busway in Birmingham, opened in 1984 and served by West Midlands Metrobuses with Tracline branding. It was the first guided busway in the world to be used by double-deckers, but closed in 1987 because in the new commercial environment the organisation was unwilling to invest in further technical development.

The privatisation of the PTEs' bus businesses was spread out over six years and all were sold to management-led employee buy-outs. The first was Yorkshire Rider, formerly West Yorkshire PTE, in 1988. The newly-privatised business expanded by buying parts of nearby AJS-owned former NBC operations. West Yorkshire (no connection with the PTE) with 120 buses was acquired in 1989 followed in 1990 by York City & District and Target Travel (90 buses), moves which took Yorkshire Rider into new territory. The company was bought by Badgerline in 1994.

Next, in 1989, was Busways Travel Services in Tyne & Wear. Busways quickly acquired the Tyne & Wear Omnibus Co, but disposed of most of its 80 buses in 1990 and made most of its employees redundant. Busways was bought by Stagecoach in 1994.

West Midlands Travel was privatised in 1991, and expanded in 1994. Locally, it took a 75 per cent stake in Your Bus, which had been set up by Smiths of Tysoe in 1987 to compete with the PTE and by 1994 was running 65 buses. But it also bought operators based far from the West Midlands, namely Westlink in west London, County Bus & Coach in Essex, and North East Bus in north-east England which operated 550 buses through its United, Tees & District and Teesside Motor Services subsidiaries.

▲ In the early 1980s the Merseyside PTE evaluated a number of new models. These included 15 Dennis Dominators, ten of which had Alexander bodies, as seen on this bus in central Liverpool. This is a 1988 photograph, when the PTE was trading as Merseybus and the advert on the side reminded travellers that it was the only operator covering the entire Merseyside region. The dot-matrix destination display was something tried by a number of operators in the 1980s, but did not see widespread use.

▼ The Greater Manchester PTE adopted this brown, orange and white livery at the end of 1980 and it was initially retained by GM Buses with the addition of a band of relief colour for each of the new company's four operating districts. The yellow band was used by the east area, with various local fleetnames – Glossop on this bus, a 1984 Leyland Olympian with 73-seat Northern Counties body.

◀ The biggest buyer of Fleetlines after London Transport was the West Midlands PTE, which took 1,209. In 1988 a 1977 Leyland-built FE30AGR with 76-seat MCW body, by then owned by West Midlands Travel, leaves the Merry Hill shopping centre in Dudley. The last of West Midland's Fleetlines were withdrawn in 1997.

➤ Busways Travel Services was the Tyne & Wear PTE's post-deregulation bus company. Busways retained the yellow and white livery inspired by Newcastle Corporation's colours, but with contrasting bands of relief. Maroon was used in Newcastle, as seen on this Alexander-bodied Atlantean, blue for South Shields and green for Sunderland. The last two acknowledged the colours of each town's municipal buses, absorbed by the PTE in 1970 and 1973 respectively.

➤ Most of the PTEs set up low-cost units as part of their deregulation strategy. These generally recruited drivers at lower wage rates than applied in the main fleet, and usually operated elderly vehicles. Blue Bus Services was a name adopted by Busways for a small part of its fleet, recalling a name once used by Newcastle Transport to market its buses, which were mainly blue until the late 1940s. In 1986 Blue Bus was running this 13-year-old Willowbrook-bodied Leyland Leopard, transferred from the main fleet.

West Midlands Travel merged with National Express in 1995, and quickly divested itself of its remote subsidiaries. Its Westlink operation was sold to London United in 1995, and its north-east of England and Essex businesses were sold to Cowie in 1996.

There was more local expansion with the purchase of Merry Hill Minibuses, formed in 1988 by the developers of the Merry Hill shopping centre near Dudley. West Midlands Travel had taken a stake in the business soon after it started and purchased it in 1997.

Three more PTE bus companies joined the private sector in 1993 in management-led employee buy-outs – Merseyside, Mainline in South Yorkshire and Strathclyde Buses, centred on Glasgow. Strathclyde expanded significantly in 1994 with the purchase of Kelvin Central Buses. It sold out to FirstBus in 1996. Mainline, too, sold out to First, in 1998. MTL Holdings, the new owner of Merseybus, expanded by buying local competitors Fareway and Liverbus. It also moved in on London, buying London Northern, London Suburban (a sister company of Liverbus) and R&I. The London operations were sold to Metroline in 1998. The Merseyside business was bought by Arriva in 2000.

That left Greater Manchester Buses. In 1993 it was split into two – GM Buses North and GM Buses South. They were each bought by their respective management/employee teams in 1994. In 1996 GMBN was bought by FirstBus and GMBS was bought by Stagecoach. ■

▼ Three years later, a rather different kind of blue bus in a very basic livery was plying the Streets of Newcastle. This ex-West Yorkshire Bristol LH, then 15 years old, was one of numerous similar buses pressed into service by Tyne & Wear Omnibus Co, which was created by Trimdon Motor Services to compete with Busways. This example was probably smarter than most when photographed in Jesmond in June 1989. By the following year Busways had taken over, and the often scruffy LHs had largely disappeared.

◄ ▼ The South Yorkshire PTE formed South Yorkshire Transport as its bus operating business. Its favoured bus in the 1980s was the Dennis Dominator, of which it became the biggest British buyer, building up a fleet of 323, which accounted for a third of all British Dominator sales. Initially SYT added red to brighten up the previous cream and brown livery, as seen on the 1981 Dominator (left), photographed in Sheffield in 1987. Later SYT's fleet received its colourful Mainline livery, as seen on the 1982 Dominator (below), photographed in Sheffield in 1997. Like most SYT Dominators, both have Alexander bodywork.

▲ At the end of 1987 Merseybus experimented with a two-tone green livery to replace the green and cream which had been used by the PTE. Around 30 buses were repainted in these colours before the decision was made to adopt maroon and cream, which became the fleet standard. The two liveries are seen in central Liverpool on Alexander-bodied Atlanteans dating from 1972 (left) and 1981 (right).

► Fareway started operations in Liverpool in 1987, initially using 15 ex-Merseyside PTE Bristol VRTs, to which it later added other types. This former Manchester Fleetline was new in 1973 and is seen in the city centre in 1988. In the background stands the 410ft-tall 1969 St John's Beacon, which originally housed a revolving restaurant. In 1993 Fareway, running 70 buses, was taken over by MTL, the privatised successor to the PTE's bus business.

Leeds City Transport was one of the pioneers in the use of panoramic windows on double-deckers and developed this style of body with Roe, whose factory was at Crossgates on the edge of the city. The 78-seat two-door body was built on long-wheelbase Daimler Fleetline and Leyland Atlantean chassis until 1974, when the PTE switched to shorter 9.5m-long Atlanteans and Fleetlines. Most of these later buses had a standard style of Roe body with one door and 76 seats. This is 1989, with a 1974 Atlantean from the final batch of long buses. It is in Yorkshire Rider livery in Leeds.

◄ In Manchester the biggest single threat to the PTE's GM Buses operation came from United Transport, which in the first half of 1987 introduced 225 new minibuses to services in south Manchester and Stockport. These included 175 Freight Rover Sherpas with 18-seat Carlyle bodies. The business was bought by Ribble in 1988 and passed on to Drawlane in 1989, at which point United Transport's planned high-quality minibus network quickly descended into being just another post-deregulation operation running assorted second-hand buses.

▲ In 1991 Busways, at this point owned by its employees, bought 20 Scania N113s with Alexander bodies – ten PS-type single-deckers and ten R-type double-deckers. They joined 26 N113 single-deckers purchased in 1989. This is the Quayside in Newcastle, with a Scania heading east to Wallsend.

▼ The Alexander P-type body was transformed into the successful PS-type with the adoption of curved windscreens and longer side windows. The combination of Volvo B10M chassis and Alexander PS-type body was favoured by Mainline between 1990 and 1996, during which time it bought 180. A 1990 bus, seen when new, loads in Sheffield city centre.

▲ Before West Midlands Travel placed Leyland's single-biggest order for Lynxes – 250 of them – its predecessor, the West Midlands PTE, had in 1986 bought six Lynxes and six Alexander-bodied Volvo B10Ms for evaluation. This is a 1990 view in Wolverhampton bus station, showing a Volvo in the colours of PTE-owned West Midlands Travel. The original Alexander P-type body with its angular flat-glass windscreens was a relatively rare type.

◄ Yorkshire Rider's operational area extended north to Harrogate when it took over the AJS-owned West Yorkshire business in 1989. This is a 1990 view, with one of 35 ex-West Yorkshire Bristol VRTs freshly repainted in Yorkshire Rider colours. This bus was new in 1980. It was unusual to find a standard NBC VRT in a former PTE fleet.

▼ Strathclyde Buses retained the orange and black livery which had been introduced by the PTE in 1983. Atlanteans featured in the fleet until 1998. In 1994 two pause at a junction in Glasgow's Argyle Street, with a Volvo Citybus in the background. The lead Atlantean was new in 1980 and like all the Atlanteans bought new by the PTE and Glasgow Corporation before, it has bodywork by Alexander.

▲ Andrews was one of the many small operators in Sheffield after deregulation, running buses in this bright livery. Often small city operators used buses discarded by the major operator, and that is the case with this ECW-bodied Daimler Fleetline which had been new to the South Yorkshire PTE in 1975. The Andrews business, running 50 buses, was bought by Yorkshire Traction in 1992. The advert on the side promotes the company's PSV and HGV driver training.

◄ Catch-a-bus was the novel name used by Hylton Castle Coaches for local bus services in South Shields. Its fleet in 1996 included this 20-year-old Leyland Leopard which had been new to Lancashire United Transport. It has a Plaxton Derwent body.

➤ By the early 1990s the level of competition between bus operators in most of Britain's towns and cities had reduced dramatically from the early years of deregulation. That made a battle between two former PTE bus businesses all the more unusual. The action was kicked off by newly-privatised MTL in 1993 when under the name MTL Manchester it started services between Manchester, Bury and Rochdale with 14 Leyland Atlanteans.

Both GM Buses North and GM Buses South responded by introducing services in Merseyside, with GM Buses South using the name Birkenhead & District and a livery inspired by the one that had been used by Birkenhead Corporation Transport. *Above right*, an MTL Manchester East Lancs-bodied Atlantean is seen in Manchester city centre in 1994. *Right*, this GM Buses South Leyland Fleetline is leaving Liverpool for a trip through the Mersey Tunnel to New Brighton.

The competition ended in 1995 when all three operators retreated to their core territories.

◀ Mayne of Manchester was an old-established operator which expanded after deregulation. It continued its policy of buying new buses, taking 16 Scania N113 double-deckers between 1989 and 2000. Most had East Lancs bodies, as on this 1996 bus with a Cityzen body approaching Mayne's city centre terminus at Piccadilly Gardens. Mayne also bought Scania coaches in the 1990s.

Between 1994 and 1996 MTL bought 110 Volvo B10Bs with Wright bodies. This is 1995 and a 12-month-old bus with Lancashire Travel fleetnames leaves Liverpool for Leigh, 25 miles away, followed by a brand new example on a local Merseybus route to Garston. St George's Hall provides the backdrop.

◄ Liverbus was a relative latecomer in Liverpool, starting up in 1990 with a fleet of former Greater Manchester Atlanteans. It bought six new Volvos in late 1994 and early 1995, two of which were Olympians with Northern Counties Palatine II bodies. The company was bought by MTL in April 1995.

▼ GM Buses was split into two companies for privatisation. GM Buses South ended up in the ownership of Stagecoach, which introduced various standard types to the fleet including Alexander-bodied Volvo Olympians. GM Buses North became part of First, which was slower to invest and whose overall orange MCW Metrobus compares unfavourably with the brightly-liveried Olympian. This is 1998. The Olympian was new to Stagecoach Oxford in 1997; the Metrobus to the Greater Manchester PTE in 1981.

➤ The spirit of co-ordination was alive and well in 1985 when the South Yorkshire PTE produced this 414-page area timetable with details of bus and train services in Barnsley and Doncaster and featuring a 1982 Yorkshire Traction Leyland National 2 on the cover. It has been repainted in a dedicated livery for the hourly Fastline X20 service linking Barnsley and Doncaster.

LEYLAND LION

Volvo had introduced a prototype of its B10M-based underfloor-engined Citybus double-decker in 1982. By the start of 1985 there were seventy in service – not a fantastic number, but enough to goad Leyland into action, in part because it was worried about losing out to Volvo with two significant customers, the Scottish Bus Group and Nottingham City Transport, both of which had taken delivery of Citybuses.

Leyland's response was the Lion. It was built in Denmark by Leyland-DAB and was powered by a horizontal Leyland TL11H engine driving through a ZF automatic gearbox. In production from 1986 to 1988 the Lion was indeed bought by the two operators whose business Leyland was anxious to retain, but no others showed any interest and just 32 were built.

An odd little twist in the story of these underfloor-engined models is that Volvo imported components from Sweden to build the Citybus in Britain, while Leyland exported components from Britain to build the Lion in Denmark.

Lion buyers

Nottingham City Transport	13
Clydeside Scottish	6
Eastern Scottish	13

Leyland's Danish-built Lion chassis found just two customers, Nottingham City Transport and the Scottish Bus Group. The first SBG Lions (above) were ten delivered to Eastern Scottish in the summer of 1986. They had Alexander R-type bodies with 86 coach seats. One leaves Glasgow on the slow service to Edinburgh via Bellshill in August 1986. Three with two-door 85-seat Northern Counties bodies were the first for Nottingham, delivered towards the end of 1986; the one below is passing Old Market Square. Note the sliding cab door and the use of the same curved glass windscreens on both decks.

5
Vanishing municipals

Leicester City Transport was running around 30 Leyland Titans in 1980. The last 20 entered service in 1967, with the bodywork order divided equally between East Lancs and, as on this bus, Metro-Cammell. This photograph was taken in Humberstone Gate in 1982, the last year of Titan operation in Leicester.

It seems quaint now, but alongside the provision of gas, electricity, water, education and sanitation, local transport was at one time a civic responsibility in almost 100 towns and cities around the UK. In 1960 there were 95 municipal transport departments running buses in Britain, each with its own livery and its own, sometimes distinctive, vehicle policy. The number of municipal bus fleets had fallen to 49 by 1980, following the formation of the seven passenger transport executives between 1969 and 1974. The municipal fleets ranged in size from Lothian Region Transport, serving Edinburgh with 600 vehicles, to tiny Colwyn Borough Council with three.

Colwyn simply ceased running buses in 1985. So did East Staffordshire District Council in Burton-on-Trent. In this case a controlling interest in the operation was taken by nearby independent Stevensons of Uttoxeter – making this in effect the first council sell-off during the period.

The remainder of the surviving 49 operations were reformed in 1986 as council-owned limited companies, a requirement of the 1985 Transport Act which deregulated local bus services.

In most towns and cities the bus fleets continued with little change to the vehicles' liveries. Notable exceptions included Chesterfield Transport, which in 1987 adopted a bright blue, yellow and white scheme to replace its conservative and old-established green and cream. Even more remarkable was Maidstone Borough Transport, which was unusual for that time in calling in a professional design consultancy, Ray Stenning's Best Impressions. Out went Maidstone's uninspiring light brown and cream, replaced with a vibrant combination of blue and yellow with a bold new name, Boro'line Maidstone.

The rebranded business was short-lived. It expanded by winning London Regional Transport tenders and its fleet more than doubled in size from 50 in 1987 to 130 in 1990. But it all went wrong and in

▲ Chester City Transport had standardised on Guy Arabs for its double-deck fleet from 1953 to 1969, by which point it had bought 47. Nine were still in use in 1980, including this 1965 bus with 73-seat Massey body. The last of Chester's Guys were replaced by Dennis Dominators in 1982. The hotel name is a nice coincidence; by the time this picture was taken both Albion and Guy had long since been absorbed into what became British Leyland.

▼ Hull was an early user of Leyland Atlanteans, taking its first in 1961 and then continuing to buy Atlanteans until 1975 when it switched to MCW Metropolitans before buying one final batch of Atlanteans in 1982. Most had Roe bodies, and those delivered between 1966 and 1969 had this unusual single-piece flat-glass windscreen, angled slightly to minimise internal reflections which might affect the driver's view at night.

➤ Between 1975 and 1981 Lincoln City Transport bought 21 Bristol VRTs with bodywork by East Lancs and, as seen here, ECW. The vast majority of Bristol VRTs had lowheight ECW bodies, and the few with full-height bodies looked a bit ungainly. Lincoln Cathedral sits high above the city centre. This is a 1985 view.

➤ Cleveland Transit was running Atlanteans, Fleetlines and VRTs in 1980. The Fleetlines included this Northern Counties-bodied bus, new in 1971 to Cleveland predecessor Teesside Municipal Transport. It was an early example of a Fleetline with a Leyland engine. The fleet number had an L prefix indicating the bus could pass under the low bridge at Middlesbrough Station where the clearance was 13ft 6in.

1992 the London operations with 57 buses were sold to Kentish Bus, while those in Maidstone were simply closed. Not so much Boro'line; more the end of the line.

It was by no means alone in this fate. Many local authority fleets were soon suffering in the maelstrom of competition which characterised the early days of deregulation. Barrow Borough Transport faced competition from Ribble and at the end of 1988 entered administration. Stagecoach bought Ribble in the spring of 1989 and a few weeks later also bought the Barrow operations from the administrators.

Stagecoach's deregulation tactics were sometimes controversial. In 1993 Lancaster City Council announced it would sell its bus operation. Stagecoach then registered a network of services covering much of Lancaster. Consequently Lancaster City Transport closed in 1994.

Also in 1994, Darlington Borough Council decided to sell its bus business. Stagecoach was one of three potential bidders, but instead of buying the company Stagecoach registered competing services using a fleet of 50 buses drafted in from some of its other subsidiaries and drivers recruited from Darlington Transport, which then closed. This move provoked widespread indignation and even alarm around the industry, but speculation about a possible reprieve for Darlington through legal intervention came to nothing.

By 2000 Stagecoach had in one way or another taken over the operations of ten former municipal businesses: Barrow-in-Furness in 1989; Cynon Valley, Grimsby Cleethorpes and Lancaster in 1993; Cleveland, Hull and Hartlepool in 1994; Chesterfield in 1995; and finally Burnley & Pendle and Hyndburn in 1996. It also owned Portsmouth City Transport between 1989 and 1991.

One municipal fleet briefly entered the private sector before being re-municipalised. Fylde Borough Transport was bought by its management in December 1993 but after just six months was sold to neighbouring council-owned Blackpool Transport in May 1994.

There were seven local authority fleets in South Wales in 1986 – Cardiff, Cynon Valley, Inter Valley Link, Islwyn, Merthyr Tydfil, Newport and Taff Ely. The two biggest, Cardiff and Newport, survived in local authority ownership, as did Islwyn, but the four other small fleets fared less well. The first to go, in 1988, was Taff Ely which served Pontypridd. It was losing money and was bought by National Welsh, a former NBC subsidiary which had been privatised in a management buy-out in 1987. In 1989 it was followed into National Welsh ownership by another loss-making operation, Inter Valley Link, owned by Rhymney Valley District Council. At Merthyr Tydfil Transport the future was looking bright in 1987 with investment in new Leyland Lynxes and a crisp new white and blue livery. But after two years of strong competition the company closed. The last of the

▼ Nottingham was the last municipal operator to specify bodywork to its own design. This 1974 Leyland Atlantean with East Lancs body is typical, although broadly similar bodies were built by Northern Counties, and alongside the Atlanteans Nottingham also bought Fleetlines. The curved windscreens on both decks and the hefty front bumper were hallmarks of the Nottingham design, but the key point was seating capacity: thanks to careful design of the interior this bus had two doors and 78 seats, at a time when most new single-door double-deckers seated around 74 passengers.

▲ Plymouth stopped buying double-decker buses in 1982. The last three delivered were its only Leyland Olympians, and had bodywork by East Lancs, like the Atlanteans that preceded them. This example was numerically the first, and is seen on a rain-battered day in September 1984. Two Volvo Citybus double-deck coaches followed, but then midibuses and single-deckers became the norm. It would be 30 years before double-decker buses made a reappearance in the fleet.

In the early 1970s Northampton Transport was buying single-deckers and it was not until 1977 that it started operating rear-engined double-deckers. These were Bristol VRTs with Alexander bodies, a relatively uncommon combination specified only by Northampton, Cardiff and Tayside. By the end of 1978 there were 40 in service, making up half of the Northampton fleet and indicative of how the government's bus grant was helping many operators to modernise their fleets. This is a 1990 view.

four to go was Cynon Valley Transport of Aberdare; it was bought in 1992 by Western Travel. This company owned former NBC business Cheltenham & Gloucester, and in 1991 had bought the neighbouring eastern area operations of National Welsh, which included services around Aberdare.

But there were success stories, too. Grampian Transport was an early privatisation, being bought by its management and employees in 1989. It set up GRT Holdings which expanded in 1990 by buying the Scottish Bus Group's Midland Scottish business. GRT headed south in 1993, when it acquired the Leicester and Northampton municipal fleets. Expansion gathered pace with the purchase of Lowland Omnibuses, Eastern Scottish and Eastern Counties, and by 1995 GRT was running 1,600 vehicles – a significant achievement for what had once been Aberdeen Corporation Transport. It then merged with Badgerline to form FirstBus, becoming one of Britain's biggest bus operators. To its portfolio of former local authority fleets First would add Great Yarmouth and Portsmouth in 1996, followed by Southampton in 1997.

British Bus, the forerunner of Arriva, acquired Stevensons of Uttoxeter in 1994, gaining full control of the Burton operations that had featured in the first council disposal. This meant that by 2000 these were in Arriva ownership, as were the former local authority fleets in Derby, Colchester and Southend.

▲ Widnes Corporation bought 11 Bristol REs with Leyland engines and East Lancs bodies between 1971 and 1973, and a further four were delivered in 1975 to its successor, Halton Borough Transport. Halton then switched to Leyland Nationals, helping to confirm the fears of bodybuilders such as East Lancs that the integral National would adversely affect their businesses. This is a short RESL, new in 1972 and seen in Widnes in 1985.

Two-door Alexander-bodied AN68 Atlanteans were the standard at Portsmouth City Transport from 1972 to 1979, during which time 90 were delivered. The Alexander AL-type body typically had curved glass windscreens on the upper deck but a number of operators, including Portsmouth, opted for flat glass which was cheaper to replace in the event of an accident. This bus was new in 1975 and is seen in central Portsmouth ten years later.

Other sales of note included two buy-outs, at Lincoln and Tayside, which were subsequently bought by Yorkshire Traction and National Express respectively. Yorkshire Traction already owned Lincolnshire Road Car, so the purchase of Lincoln City Transport consolidated its position in the area. Tayside, which provided local services in the Dundee area, became National Express's only significant bus operation outside its home territory in the West Midlands. A third buy-out to be sold on to a major group was Brighton Borough Transport, bought by its employees in 1993 and sold to Go-Ahead in 1997. Go-Ahead already owned the former NBC Brighton & Hove company so, as with Yorkshire Traction in Lincoln, was consolidating its position.

From 49 fleets in local authority ownership in 1980, the number had fallen to 17 in 2000. Lothian, now with 510 buses and coaches, was still the biggest. The smallest was Islwyn, with 41. The accompanying table provides a summary of the changes in ownership of Britain's local authority fleets. This was by no means the end of the story; 20 years later, the number had shrunk by a further ten, leaving just seven in public ownership. ■

▲ Cynon Valley Transport adopted this livery in 1986 when one-time Halifax Corporation general manager Geoffrey Hilditch was appointed managing director. The colours were similar to those used by Halifax until its absorption by the West Yorkshire PTE in 1974. An ECW-bodied Bristol RE heads through Aberdare in 1988.

▼ This table lists the 49 municipal transport fleets in Britain in 1980. The *Initial sale* column shows who originally bought those fleets which were privatised, and identifies those which were closed down in the aftermath of deregulation. The *Ownership in 2000* column indicates the position in 2000. Over the years route networks were frequently revised so that in many towns the bus services in 2000 owed little or nothing to the former municipal operation.

Local authority bus fleet summary

Operator	1980 fleet	Initial sale	Ownership in 2000
Aberconwy	8	closed, 1999	-
Barrow-in-Furness	56	Stagecoach, 1989	Stagecoach
Blackburn	90	-	still local authority owned
Blackpool	129	-	still local authority owned
Bournemouth	155	-	still local authority owned
Brighton	67	buy-out, 1993	Go-Ahead, 1997
Burnley & Pendle	124	Stagecoach, 1996	Stagecoach
Cardiff	218	-	still local authority owned
Chester	60	-	still local authority owned
Chesterfield	123	buy-out, 1990	Stagecoach, 1995
Cleveland Transit	257	buy-out, 1991	Stagecoach, 1994
Colchester	62	British Bus, 1993	Arriva
Colwyn	3	closed, 1985	-
Cynon Valley	36	Western Travel, 1992	Stagecoach, 1993
Darlington	77	closed, 1994	-
Derby	142	employees/Luton & District, 1989	Arriva via British Bus, 1994
East Staffordshire	42	Stevensons of Uttoxeter, 1985	Arriva via British Bus, 1994
Eastbourne	62	-	still local authority owned
Fylde	42	buy-out, 1993	bought by Blackpool, 1994
Grampian	227	buy-out, 1989	First via GRT
Great Yarmouth	62	First, 1996	First
Grimsby Cleethorpes	97	Stagecoach, 1993	Stagecoach
Halton	40	-	still local authority owned
Hartlepool	84	buy-out, 1993	Stagecoach, 1994
Hull	248	employees/Cleveland Transit, 1993	Stagecoach, 1994
Hyndburn	54	Stagecoach, 1996	Stagecoach
Inter-Valley Link	68	National Welsh, 1989	closed, 1992
Ipswich	75	-	still local authority owned
Islwyn	32	-	still local authority owned
Lancaster	61	closed, 1993	-
Leicester	232	GRT, 1993	First, 1995
Lincoln	48	employees/Derby City Transport, 1991	Yorkshire Traction, 1993
Lothian	601	-	still local authority owned
Maidstone Boro'line	44	closed, 1992	-
Merthyr Tydfil	66	closed, 1989	-
Newport	95	-	still local authority owned
Northampton	75	GRT, 1993	First, 1995
Nottingham	381	-	still local authority owned
Plymouth	200	-	still local authority owned
Portsmouth	159	employees/Southampton Citybus, 1988	First via Stagecoach,Transit,1996
Preston	96	buy-out, 1993	no change
Reading	133	-	still local authority owned
Rossendale	51	-	still local authority owned
Southampton	182	buy-out, 1993	First, 1997
Southend	80	British Bus, 1993	Arriva
Taff-Ely	39	National Welsh, 1988	closed, 1992
Tayside	195	buy-out, 1991	National Express, 1997
Thamesdown	70	-	still local authority owned
Warrington	83	-	still local authority owned

Barrow was another customer lost by East Lancs with the arrival of the Leyland National. The Leopard in the background is one of ten East Lancs-bodied buses delivered in 1968–69, while the National in the foreground represents 16 bought between 1974 and 1980. Barrow was the closest local authority fleet to the National factory in Workington, which was 70 miles to the north up the Cumbrian coast.

Seddon introduced the rear-engined Pennine RU bus in 1969, offering it as a complete vehicle with Seddon-built bodywork, and as a chassis for other builders to body. Though never widely popular, it did win some fleet orders, most notably 100 for NBC's Crosville fleet, and it appealed to a number of municipal buyers such as Darlington, which took eight in the winter of 1973–74. They were among the last RUs produced. One is seen in the town in 1984, carrying a warning to passengers that they have to pay the exact fare. The free-standing 1864 clock tower behind the bus was designed by renowned architect Alfred Waterhouse.

▲ Leicester was one of the biggest buyers of the Dennis Dominator, building up a fleet of 144. Most had East Lancs bodies, as on this 1982 bus. The red, white and grey livery was introduced in 1984 and was used on all municipal vehicles. It was replaced in 1990 when a traditional and rather sombre maroon and cream livery was reintroduced, echoing a style used on the city's buses in the period up to 1961.

➤ Blackpool Transport bought 65 long-wheelbase Leyland Atlanteans with East Lancs bodies between 1977 and 1984. Most of them were 86-seat buses, as seen here with a four-year-old example in the evening sunlight on the promenade in 1987.

East Staffordshire District Council was among the smallest local authority fleets in England in 1980, with 42 buses. These included ten Fleetlines delivered to its predecessor, Burton-upon-Trent, with Willowbrook bodies based on the idiosyncratic design developed by Nottingham City Transport. They replaced 25 per cent of the fleet. This photograph was taken in Burton in July 1985; in October East Staffordshire's bus operations were merged with those of independent Stevensons of Uttoxeter, which took control of the combined operation.

▼ Lothian Region Transport moved seamlessly from Leyland Atlanteans in 1981 to Leyland Olympians in 1982. After evaluating two standard-wheelbase buses with Alexander bodies, Lothian ordered four batches of long-wheelbase Olympians with Leyland TL11 engines. The bodies were supplied by ECW, which caused some consternation at nearby Alexander, Lothian's traditional body supplier. In 1988, following the closure of ECW, Lothian's body orders reverted to Alexander. A 1983 Olympian is seen in Princes Street in 1984.

▲ The Bedford JJL integral midibus had a Marshall body styled by Vauxhall which, like Bedford, was part of General Motors. It had a rear-mounted 5.4-litre Bedford engine and an Allison automatic gearbox. The JJL was 7.5m long and had 24 seats. Four prototypes were built and operated as Bedford demonstrators and three of them spent some time in the Brighton Borough Transport fleet. One climbs North Street in 1987 on a central area shuttle service.

▼ At the end of the 1960s MCW and Scania teamed up to build a British version of the Scania CR110 city bus, which was marketed as the Metro-Scania and was intended as a competitor for the Leyland National. Between 1971 and 1973 MCW sold 131, with the biggest buyers being the municipal fleets of Newport with 44 and Leicester with 35. A Newport bus, new in 1972, leaves the town's bus station in 1989.

▲ Among the biggest buses to enter local authority service in the 1980s were Boro'line Maidstone's two Scania K92s with 92-seat East Lancs bodies. They were new in 1987. The boxy body design was not to everyone's taste, but its sheer size was certainly striking, and the stunning livery more than compensated for any shortcomings in style. Only four K92s were bodied as double-deckers; the other two were for Grey-Green of London and also had East Lancs bodies but with a more stylish front end.

Until 1980 Grimsby Cleethorpes Transport was buying Fleetlines. It took one batch of Leyland Olympians in 1984, then standardised on the Dennis Dominator, taking 15 between 1989 and 1992. This was the operator's first Dominator, with 78-seat Alexander body. It was photographed in May 1989, a few weeks after entering service.

◄ By the end of the 1980s Nottingham City Transport was running 36 Volvo Citybuses with the undertaking's distinctive bodywork. This bus was new in 1985 and had 84-seat two-door Northern Counties bodywork, which was clearly related to the 1974 East Lancs-bodied Atlantean illustrated on page 47 – though the deeper upper-deck windscreen on these later bodies gave them a more imposing appearance. This is a 1998 view in Market Square.

◄ Cardiff City Transport was the biggest buyer of Bristol VRTs outside the National Bus Company, with 117 being delivered between 1974 and 1980. They had bodywork by ECW, Willowbrook and, as on this 1978 bus, Alexander. The offside fleetname is in Welsh, Bws Caerdydd. This is 1989.

The disc on the front of this Southampton CityBus Leyland Atlantean in 1989 reads, "We are your bus company," stressing the ownership of the company by the city council as it faced competition from other operators. In 1993 the business was bought by its employees. Southampton standardised on East Lancs-bodied Atlanteans from 1968 to 1982. This was a 1978 delivery.

TRAVEL MAP & GUIDE 1993

SOUTHAMPTON Citybus

We put the bus in business

YOUR HANDY GUIDE

▲ Most Dennis Falcons were bought by municipal fleets. These included Chesterfield, which took nine in 1983–84. Marshall bodywork was fitted to the five delivered in 1984. When new this bus was in Chesterfield's traditional green and cream but when photographed in June 1990, just after the employee buy-out of the business in April, it was in the brighter colours adopted in 1987.

➤ When Islwyn Borough Transport bought small buses in 1987 it didn't go for any of the obvious choices but instead ordered six Perkins-engined Dodge G08 chassis which were fitted with 25-seat East Lancs bodies, creating a unique batch of buses. The G08 truck was a popular choice among local authorities, but very few were bodied as PSVs. One of these unusual buses pulls out of Blackwood bus station in 1995.

The only Leyland Olympians bodied by Marshall were 20 for Bournemouth Transport in 1982. They were 78-seaters with Gardner engines.

▼ Warrington Borough Transport bought 19 Dennis Dominators between 1982 and 1989, all with East Lancs bodies. The last eight featured the bodybuilder's coach-style front end. Two of the 1989 buses are seen in Warrington town centre in 1995.

▲ While most of Warrington's buses were red, a blue livery was used in the early 1990s on coaches and on Dennis Darts with MidiLines branding. Ten Darts delivered in the winter of 1993–94 had 35-seat Northern Counties bodies. They featured a split-level entrance designed to make boarding easier for passengers with restricted mobility.

◄ Following coach deregulation Southend Transport introduced limited-stop services to London, aimed principally at commuters. The most impressive vehicles in its coach fleet were five 12m-long 84-seat Van Hool Astromegas. They had 14.6-litre Mercedes-Benz OM422 V8 engines and Allison automatic gearboxes.

▲ Thamesdown Transport started buying Dennis Darts with Plaxton Pointer bodies in 1993 and by 2000 was running 54, all with Dartline branding. The later vehicles were low-entry SLF models, as illustrated by this 1996 bus. There were eight buses in this batch, numbered 151–158, and all had matching P-prefix registration numbers except for this bus, 155, because the DVLA was not prepared to risk causing offence by issuing a registration with the combination P155...

▼ The integral Optare Excel was a Dart rival. In 1997 Ipswich Buses bought ten 11.5m Excels with 37 or 38 seats, alongside three Dart SLFs with 42-seat East Lancs bodies. More of each type would join the fleet. The red ribbon under the windscreen carries the name "Chantry Infant School".

▲ When demand for new bus bodies was at a low point at the start of the 1990s East Lancs developed a market for refurbished Leyland Nationals, creating a product which it marketed as the Greenway. The basic body structure was retained but with a new interior and major changes to the exterior. Most Greenways were fitted with Gardner engines, and there was a choice of gearboxes. Seven joined the fleet of Colchester Borough Transport in 1996, at which time it was a subsidiary of British Bus but retained a distinct local identity. The Greenways had been transferred from sister British Bus company London & Country and were rebuilds of buses which had been new to various NBC companies. One climbs East Hill on its approach to the town centre in 1998.

Production of the integral Leyland National got under way at a brand new factory in Workington in Cumberland in 1971. The model was re-engineered in 1979 as the National 2 to accommodate the Leyland 680 engine in place of the original and unpopular 500-series. But sales never achieved the volumes Leyland had hoped for. The factory was designed to build 2,000 buses a year but at its peak produced just under half that number. Between 1982 and 1985 annual production was down to just double figures, falling to only 33 in the last of those years.

The Lynx was a quite different beast from the integral National, having a separate underframe. However, would-be customers in Britain were still required to buy the whole vehicle from Leyland, as they had been with the National, since it was only offered to them with Leyland's own integrated body structure. To increase sales in export markets the intention was that the Lynx underframe would be made available to local bodybuilders, but in the event the only significant 'export' order was for six Lynxes which were bodied by Alexander Belfast for operation in Northern Ireland.

Also unlike the National, the Lynx was launched with a choice of engines. Leyland wanted buyers to specify its TL11H, the turbocharged successor to the 680 fitted to most National 2s. But bowing to customer pressure it also offered the Gardner 6HLXB and 6HLXCT and, when it became apparent that there was no long-term future for the TL11H, the Cummins L10.

Production started at Workington in 1986. The first Cummins-powered buses were built in late 1987 and the last Lynxes with TL11H engines rolled out of the factory in the middle of 1988. Sales were slow at the start, reflecting the depressed demand for big buses in the early years of deregulation. Significant early orders included 18 from Merthyr Tydfil Transport in 1987, followed by 50 from Caldaire at the start of 1988 and 30 from Eastern National later in the same year. Nottingham City Transport took 20 between April 1988 and January 1989. Bristol received 62 in 1989–90.

But this was happening against a challenging background. Leyland Bus was bought by its management in 1987 and then taken over by Volvo in 1988. However the Lynx survived and in 1989 secured its biggest order, 250 for West Midlands Travel, at that time still owned by the PTE.

Volvo envisaged a long-term future for the Lynx, and towards the end of 1990 unveiled the Lynx II. This had various updates, the most obvious of which was a revised front panel. This provided space for a bigger radiator which Volvo thought might be needed on some variants powered by its own THD102 engine, although only 15 Lynxes were built with Volvo engines.

Production of the Lynx came to an end in 1992. It was replaced by the Volvo B10B.

➤ Bristol Omnibus was among the more enthusiastic Lynx buyers, taking 62 in 1989–90. This is one of the first, and is seen in central Bristol soon after delivery in summer 1989.

The Lynx II was easily identifiable by its revised front end. United Auto received this one in 1991. This is Newcastle with the massive brutalist Newgate multi-storey car park as a backdrop.

LYNX

THE · NEW · GENERATION · CITY · BUS

In 1989 Southampton Citybus acquired three Lynxes, then the following year it added another ten, of which this is one. It is seen leaving the bus stands in Vincents Walk in July 1990.

6
Big groups dominate in Scottish privatisation

Characterising SBG's fresh approach to its Glasgow operations after deregulation are these ex-London Routemasters in the Clydeside fleet. They are approaching Buchanan Bus Station on two suburban routes which both competed with PTE-owned Strathclyde Buses. Clydeside operated Routemasters from 1985 to 1990.

Scottish Bus Group, like NBC, was state-owned. Its services in 1980 covered the country from John o'Groats to the English border. These were provided by seven subsidiary companies which between them ran 3,700 buses and coaches. While local authority operators held sway in the country's four biggest cities (Glasgow, Edinburgh, Aberdeen and Dundee), SBG had a strong presence in all of them, and in most other towns and cities it was the principal operator.

The Group reorganised its bus-operating subsidiaries in June 1985, creating 11 companies whose territories were more closely aligned with the boundaries of the regional councils. The results of the changes were:

▲ Northern Scottish served the Grampian region of north-east Scotland. An Alexander-bodied Leyland Leopard leaves Aberdeen bus station, joining congested evening peak traffic in 1985 as it starts its journey to Dundee, some 70 miles to the south.

▼ SBG adopted standardised fleetnames across all its subsidiaries in 1978, although this Western Seddon Pennine VII was still carrying an earlier and more flamboyant style when seen leaving Glasgow's Anderston Bus Station for Ayr in 1986. While Western's buses were red, its coaches were black and white with grey relief.

| COMPANY | FLEET SIZE 1985 | |
	Before 17 June	After 17 June
Central	494	474
Clydeside	-	334
Eastern	554	367
Fife	300	300
Highland	228	208
Kelvin	-	380
Lowland	-	104
Midland	599	292
Northern	317	254
Strathtay	-	126
Western	659	317
Total	**3,151**	**3,156**

The new organisation also readied the Group for the competition which appeared with local bus deregulation in 1986. SBG expanded aggressively

in Glasgow and Edinburgh, competing with the local authority Strathclyde and Lothian fleets.

In Aberdeen a joint network had been established between Alexander Northern and Grampian Regional Transport in 1983, with Northern buses on city services being repainted in Grampian livery. That co-operation ended with deregulation, and Northern and Grampian became competitors.

SBG's deregulation strategy was not an unqualified success. It suffered particularly badly in the Glasgow area, where PTE-owned Strathclyde Buses mounted a spirited defence of its territory. The two new companies running in Glasgow, Clydeside and Kelvin, had short lives.

As elsewhere in Britain new operators appeared. The most successful was Stagecoach – then still a small business – which introduced local services in Glasgow and Perth in 1986 and

▲ The Ailsa had been developed by Volvo's British truck importer to meet SBG's demands for a bus which would be more reliable than its rear-engined Daimler Fleetlines and Bristol VRTs. Eastern Scottish bought 30 new Ailsas. The first ten, in 1978, had this style of Alexander body. This bus is leaving Edinburgh bus station in St Andrew Square.

SBG sales

Clydeside	
Western	1991
management	1991
British Bus	1994
Arriva	1997
Eastern	
management	1990
GRT	1993
First	1995
Fife	
Stagecoach	1991
Highland	
Clansman/Rapson	1991
Highland Country	1995
Citylink	1996
Rapson	1998
Highland Scottish	1995
Rapson	
Kelvin Central	
management	1991
SB Holdings	1994
First	1995
Lowland	
management	1990
GRT	1993
First	1995
Midland	
GRT	1990
First	1995
Northern	
Stagecoach	1991
Strathtay	
Yorkshire Traction	1991
Western	
management	1991
Stagecoach	1994

Leyland Leopards with Alexander Y-type bodies could be seen the length and breadth of Scotland. Central Scottish ran this 53-seater, which has just passed under the approach to Glasgow Central Station as it heads to Anderston Bus Station. This bus was new in 1973, but broadly similar Leopard buses were bought by SBG between 1964 and 1982.

would over the next decade emerge as one of Scotland's biggest bus operators. But most of the competition for SBG came from new small operators, and these were often short-lived. Existing independents focused on protecting their established routes.

When the government announced in 1988 that SBG was to be privatised the group's management, supported by a majority of its employees, argued that it should be privatised as a single entity. The government disagreed and in 1990–91 the group's bus companies were sold individually. There were now nine. Clydeside, formed from Western's northern area, had been re-united with Western in 1989, and in the same year Kelvin was combined with Central.

Management-led buy-outs took control at four companies, Eastern, Kelvin Central, Lowland and Western. The former Clydeside operations were immediately sold by Western to a management and employee buy-out. Stagecoach purchased two, Northern and Fife. GRT, formed by the recently-privatised Grampian Regional Transport, secured Midland while Yorkshire Traction bought Strathtay, the only sale to an English company. Highland was bought by a combination of Clansman Travel (which had purchased SBG's Scottish Citylink express coach business) and Rapsons Coaches of Alness.

There were rapid changes in ownership. GRT added Lowland and Eastern to its portfolio in 1993, re-uniting under common ownership two companies which had been divided in 1985. Stagecoach acquired Western in 1994. ∎

▲ The launch of Scottish Citylink in 1983 improved the quality of the coaches used on SBG's express services. Most were Leyland Leopards and Tigers with Duple or Plaxton bodies, but among the more unusual types was this Alexander-bodied Seddon Pennine VII. New in 1979 it was upgraded by the fitting of reclining seats and was used by Western Scottish on the service from Glasgow to Kennacraig on the Kintyre peninsula. It is seen leaving Buchanan Bus Station in 1984.

Strathtay Scottish was created in 1985 to take over parts of SBG's Midland and Northern companies. This Alexander-bodied MCW Metrobus, new to Midland in 1982, is operating a Perth city service in 1986. Strathtay's unusual livery, regarded by some as an unsympathetic clash of colours, was later brightened by the addition of white relief.

▲ Fife Scottish built up a fleet of 74 Alexander-bodied Ailsas. New in 1979 and seen the following year, this is a MkII model with a higher driving position than on the original. The location is Dunfermline bus station.

SBG vehicle policy

The most common type of vehicle in SBG service in 1980 was the Alexander Y-type single-decker, most frequently based on Leyland Leopard, Ford R-series and Seddon Pennine chassis. The Leyland National, which was the dominant single-deck type in NBC, was only bought in small numbers by SBG.

SBG had found the switch from front- to rear-engined double-deckers a traumatic experience. It had settled on Daimler Fleetlines, which in 1980 made up the majority of its double-deck fleet, but it also had a number of front-engined Ailsas. This chassis had been developed by the UK importer of Volvo trucks, specifically to address SBG's concerns about the reliability (or, more correctly, the unreliability) of rear-engined models.

The last SBG Fleetlines, which went to Alexander Midland, entered service in 1980, after which SBG's double-deck orders were divided between Dennis, MCW, Leyland and Volvo, the last-named supplying Ailsas until 1984, and then the mid-engined Citybus, which was a development of the popular B10M coach chassis. SBG's MCW Metrobuses were relatively unusual in being supplied as chassis fitted with low-height bodies by Alexander rather than as integrals with MCW's own bodywork.

▲ The Leyland Olympian was the standard Northern Scottish double-decker in the 1980s, and most had Alexander R-type bodies. Seen arriving at Aberdeen bus station in 1986 when just a few weeks old, this Olympian was unusual in having coach seats. The addition of blue to Northern's yellow and cream livery provided a link with the colours of the original Alexander company which had served Aberdeen until 1961.

Highland Scottish took delivery of 15 ECW-bodied Leyland Fleetlines in 1978–79. This bus is in Drumnadrochit in 1992, a year after the company had been privatised.

For most of its ex-London AEC Routemasters Strathtay Scottish adopted this bright striped livery. The Routemasters were used on local services in Dundee, and as illustrated here in 1987, Perth. A very different approach to Strathtay's livery for Perth Routemasters is seen on page 86.

▼ In 1985 Western Scottish adapted its black, white and grey coach livery for use on buses – hinting at the company's prewar black and white bus livery. A 1979 Northern Counties-bodied Leyland Fleetline in Dumfries in 1991 shows the traditional-looking Western name which was used by the company after privatisation.

➤ To promote the sale of SBG's subsidiaries this full-page advert showed an approximation of each company's livery on a drawing of a Plaxton Paramount. The odd mixture of colours on some of the drawings suggest that the advertising agency's staff hadn't actually seen many SBG buses.

7
London: competition, but not on the streets

By 1980 most of London Transport's trouble-prone rear-engined AEC single-deckers had been withdrawn. Survivors could still be found operating the central area Red Arrow network. These included this 1971 Metro-Cammell-bodied Swift with an 8.2-litre engine – a type used primarily on suburban services, not a genuine Red Arrow Merlin with AEC's more powerful 11.3-litre unit. This bus had been withdrawn in 1978 then reinstated to run briefly on Red Arrow services. It is leaving Victoria Bus Station in the spring of 1980, heading for Waterloo. A fleet of 69 new Leyland National 2s took over the Red Arrow routes in 1981.

Bus users in London were spared the upheavals caused by deregulation. Competition did come to London, but it was competition to win tenders to run bus services, not competition for passengers between rival bus operators on the streets.

In 1980 the London Transport Executive was running almost 6,500 buses, including some 2,800 obsolescent Routemasters. Restructuring of LTE in 1985 saw responsibility for the bus fleet – by then standing at 5,500 vehicles – passing to London Buses Ltd, while its parent body, London Regional Transport, had the job of planning the routes and

▲ The changes taking place in London as a result of route tendering are encapsulated in this view at Golders Green in 1989 showing two E-registered buses. The old order is illustrated by a 22-year-old crew-operated Routemaster with an E-suffix registration from the London Northern fleet; the new order by a 12-month-old Grey-Green Scania N112 with an E-prefix registration. The Scania has a 75-seat East Lancs body broadly imitating the contemporary Alexander design and displays the LRT symbol in the windscreen to reassure passengers that although it isn't red, it is still a bus.

➤ Like the Swifts and Merlins, London Transport's Fleetlines were deemed not to be up to the job of coping with LT's tough operating conditions. This is a late model, a 1978 FE30ALR with a turbocharged Leyland 690 power unit and engine encapsulation to reduce noise. The body on this bus was by Park Royal, but near-identical bodies were also built by Metro-Cammell. It is seen at Holborn Circus in January 1981.

➤ After the unsatisfactory Fleetlines, London Transport switched to two new types where it had had input into the design – the MCW Metrobus and Leyland Titan. A 1981 Metrobus is seen in 1985 in the sylvan setting of Hammond Street, near Cheshunt, making its way from Waltham Abbey to Potters Bar. When it was new the centre grille section would have been black to match the headlamp surrounds and corner panels.

setting the fares. LRT was required to put London's bus routes out to competitive tender; the tenders were typically awarded for five years. The first tenders were awarded in 1985, and London Buses only managed to win just under half.

The remainder went to new operators and among the early providers of LRT contracted services were coach operators Len Wright Travel, Scancoach and Sampsons of Cheshunt, tour operator Cityrama, and NBC subsidiaries Eastern National and London Country. Some of the newcomers were short-lived. Sampsons, for example, had its contract terminated after two years following complaints about service reliability. Cityrama gave up its contracted services after three years.

But others thrived. London Buslines, set up by Len Wright, operated services in west London until 1996, when the business was purchased by former London Buses' subsidiary CentreWest. Grey-Green won its first LRT routes in 1987 and became the first of the new breed of London independents to win a route through central London. This was the high-profile 24, running from Hampstead to Pimlico via Trafalgar Square and Parliament Square. The Grey-Green fleet of Volvo Citybuses with their grey and green livery provided a striking reminder of the change that was under way.

There was no requirement at this stage for buses to be painted red, so for a period London was a colourful city. Among the most striking fleets were those of Boro'line Maidstone in blue and yellow, Kentish Bus in cream and maroon, R&I in blue and grey, Capital Citybus in yellow and Armchair in white and orange.

In a bid to gain an edge when competing with independent companies London Buses set up operations where costs were reduced by the adoption of different working conditions and lower pay rates – both, understandably, contentious subjects. This saw the emergence of Bexleybus, Harrow Buses, Roundabout in Orpington and Westlink in Hounslow, all of which were successful in winning tenders in the late 1980s, although not always successful in retaining them when the routes came up for re-tendering. London Buses also continued to bid for new tenders through its existing mainstream business.

Tendering was not planned as a long-term way of managing London's bus services. The government repeatedly promised that London's buses would be deregulated in line with the rest of Great Britain. One company was keen to gain London experience ahead of this happening. In 1989 Transit Holdings, which was running high-frequency urban minibus services in Devon, Oxford and Portsmouth, launched Docklands Transit, with 70 minibuses serving the rapidly-developing Docklands area. These were licensed by the Metropolitan traffic commissioner, an unusual arrangement. The services were not part of the LRT network and LRT's travelcards were not valid on them, which Docklands Transit claimed was the primary reason for the operation's sudden demise in November 1990 – a claim disputed by LRT.

Also anticipating deregulation – and privatisation – London Buses was reorganised in 1989 with the creation of eleven large bus operating units (one of which, London Forest, closed in 1991) plus London Coaches. The coach business was sold to its management in 1992; the bus companies, now running just over 4,900 vehicles, were privatised between January 1994 and January 1995. At the same time there was a reorganisation of the tendering procedure which became the responsibility of a new body, London Transport Buses.

The privatisation process saw five London Buses subsidiaries being taken over in management buy-outs and six being acquired by outside buyers:

COMPANY	FLEET SIZE	NEW OWNER
CentreWest	507	Management buy-out
East London	592	Stagecoach
Selkent	414	Stagecoach
Leaside	523	Cowie
Metroline	386	Management buy-out
London Central	498	Go-Ahead
London Northern	341	MTL London
London General	636	Management buy-out
London United	464	Management buy-out
South London	447	Cowie
Westlink	118	Management buy-out

As elsewhere in Britain there was soon a measure of consolidation. Westlink had been bought by its management in January 1994, but was sold to West Midlands Travel three months later and then resold to London United in 1995. MTL London expanded in 1995 by buying two companies in its general operating area, R&I which had been running tendered services since 1989, and London Suburban, which had started in 1993. The latter was, like MTL, based in Liverpool. MTL London in turn was bought by neighbouring Metroline in 1998. Go-Ahead, which bought London Central in 1994, purchased the adjacent London General business from its management in 1996.

At the start of 1997 FirstBus's only interest in London was Thamesway, formed in 1990 to take over the London and south Essex operations of Eastern National. In March it expanded by buying CentreWest, which was running 500 buses. Then in 1998 it bought Capital Citybus. This business had been formed in 1990 when the owners of Hong Kong Citybus had bought the LRT operations of Ensign Bus. It was the first major investment in London's bus operations by a foreign company but would not be the last: London United was bought by French group Transdev in 1998, while Metroline was purchased by DelGro, a Singapore-based transport group, in 2000.

▲ The purchase by London Buses of 82 second-hand double-deckers in the middle of the 1980s was a surprise. Even more surprising was that most of them were front-engined Ailsas, including fifty 11-year-old buses from the West Midlands PTE. One is seen in Hertford soon after entering London service in 1987. The 310A was a commercially operated service run by London Buses' Potters Bar garage.

▼ LT bought fewer Titans than Metrobuses, in part because of production delays caused by the closure of Leyland's Park Royal factory, where the original Titans were built. A 1984 London Northern Titan, produced at Leyland's Workington factory, heads north through Holloway after a summer shower in 1990. The Jones Brothers department store to the left, then owned by John Lewis, was controversially closed amid widespread local protest a month after this picture was taken.

▲ London Buses' last big double-deck order was for 260 Leyland Olympians with ECW bodies, delivered in 1986–87. In Victoria in 1992 an Olympian passes a Titan. There were points of similarity, most obvious in this view being the dark area which gives the Olympian grille a horizontal look, and the shape of the top deck windows and roof.

▲ Some unusual types of bus appeared on LRT contracted services, such as this Leyland Cub operated by Crystals of Orpington between Downe and Bromley North. Cub buses in use as PSVs were rare, and the two owned by Crystals were the only examples with Lex-HTI Maxeta bodies. Note the route number painted above the windscreen. This service had previously been operated by LT using Bristol LHs.

In 1997 there were 32 operators running buses on LTB services. Most of these buses were red because they belonged to companies which had been part of London Buses, all of which retained red as the base colour for their fleets. But there remained a colourful choice of buses around the British capital, and LTB decided it was time for change: buses on LTB contracts should have a livery which was at least 80 per cent red. The colourful era was drawing to a close.

A late and short-lived burst of colour came from Harris of Grays, which secured its first LTB contract in 1997. By 1999 it was running 76 buses on LTB services. But it was unable to square the economics of the operation, and at the end of the year it called in the receivers. This was the biggest failure of an LRT/LTB contractor since the collapse of Boro'line in 1992, when Kentish Bus took over Boro'line's contracts and 57 vehicles. Unusually, the Harris services and vehicles were taken over by LTB, trading as East Thames Buses, rather than being handed over to other contractors.

Tendering had certainly brought competition to London but in 2000, 15 years after it was introduced, just five major operators provided over 80 per cent of London's bus services as calculated by scheduled mileage:

Arriva	20.7
Go-Ahead	17.2
FirstGroup	16.7
Stagecoach	16.7
Metroline	12.0

The remaining mileage was provided by smaller operators. ■

▲ Sampsons of Cheshunt was one of the less successful LRT contractors. It won the tender for the 217B linking Enfield Town and Upshire in 1986, but had the contract rescinded in 1988 following complaints about service reliability. The livery was distinctive, as shown on an ex-South Yorkshire PTE Daimler Fleetline with ECW body in Enfield in 1987. The B suffix to the route number is displayed alongside the destination as there was no space in the three-track number display.

London vehicle policy

In the early 1980s London Transport was buying Leyland Titans, Leyland Nationals and MCW Metrobuses. The changes in operators brought changes in vehicle types. In the mid-1980s additions to the London Buses fleet included second-hand Ailsas and Metrobuses, while the organisation's last major order for new double-deckers was for 260 ECW-bodied Leyland Olympians delivered in 1986–87. More followed, to give London Buses a fleet of 354 Olympians by 1992. However, at the end of the 1980s it was also buying small buses from Mercedes-Benz, Renault and MCW. It was a dramatic change, from expensive double-deckers developed to meet London's operational requirements to mass-produced light truck chassis adapted for use as buses.

The small operators bought a wide range of vehicles, from ex-London Fleetlines in the early days to new double-deckers from Leyland, Volvo, Scania and Dennis.

Dennis experienced a remarkable boost in bus sales in London with its Dart single-decker, which was bought in large numbers by London Buses subsidiaries, as well as by many of the smaller London Transport Buses contractors.

One curiosity of the tendering regime was the survival of Routemasters, of which more than 500 were still in service in 2000. LRT remained convinced that with their conductors and their open platforms these were the best option for many of the busiest routes passing through central London; so instead of specifying new buses for these routes it took ownership of its Routemaster fleet and supplied them to operators winning tenders.

This meant Routemasters were the last legacy of the erstwhile London Transport's insistence that it needed buses designed to serve the biggest and most congested urban area in Britain – far outliving the Titans and Metrobuses, whose design LT had also sought to influence. The buses it designed itself were, we were told, paragons of reliability. The buses in whose design it had no influence were nothing but trouble. Yet London's bus operators of the 1990s were buying manufacturers' standard products, and even though congestion was as bad as it had ever been – surprise, surprise – they worked.

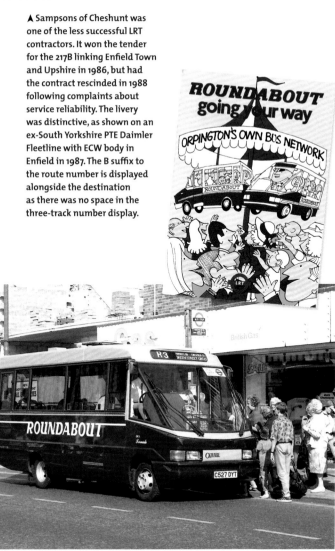

◄ One of London Buses' low-cost operations was Roundabout, the trading name for Orpington Buses. It started life in 1986 with this smart livery, seen on a stylish Optare CityPacer. The chassis was a modified MAN-VW light truck which wasn't quite up to the job of stop-start bus operation. The CityPacers were sold after five years.

While many early LRT contracts were won by independents, NBC subsidiaries also submitted bids which sometimes undercut those of London Buses. These included Eastern National, which took over an Enfield area service in 1985 using unusual short-wheelbase Bedford YMQ-S models with 33-seat Wadham Stringer bodies. These had high-backed seats, providing unaccustomed luxury to passengers who had previously been travelling on ECW-bodied Bristol LHs.

▼ Bearing in mind that until 1985 all Orpington's buses were red, this and the picture to the left give an idea of how colourful London's buses were becoming in the late 1980s. Local company Metrobus was another operator to win LRT contracts, and the buses it used on its first tendered service were 13 ex-LT Fleetlines including this smartly repainted ten-year-old example. Metrobus was still a small operator at this time and the 13 Fleetlines doubled the size of its fleet.

▲ Another NBC operator to secure LRT tenders was London Country. This is Orpington in the summer of 1986 and the bus is a 1974 ex-Strathclyde PTE Alexander-bodied Leyland Atlantean from a batch of 31 bought by London Country specifically for use on LRT contracts.

◄ London Buslines won its first LRT contracts in 1985, and gradually expanded its operations in west and north-west London as it won more tenders. At the end of 1990 it took delivery of 17 Northern Counties-bodied Leyland Olympians, some of which were for route 92 between Ealing Hospital and Neasden. They were in a new livery designed by the Best Impressions consultancy.

▼ London Buses' Harrow Buses operation started up in 1987 with a mixed fleet in a bright livery which retained a link with LT's traditional colours. New vehicles included 29 leased MCW Metrobus MkIIs which were returned to the lessor, Plaxton Coach Sales, when Harrow Buses lost a significant proportion of its contracts on re-tendering in 1990.

Drawlane subsidiary London & Country became a major contractor to LRT, principally in south-west London. This is Hounslow in 1990, with a Volvo Citybus with 88-seat East Lancs body pulling out of the bus station. It was one of 38 Citybuses delivered in 1989 to cover new LRT contracts.

▲ Unusual new types appeared in the London Buses fleet in the late 1980s. These included nine Alexander-bodied Scania N113s built as stock vehicles, a common practice adopted at that time partly to keep factories working and partly so that quick delivery could be offered on small batches of buses. These, London's first Scania double-deckers, were operated by London Northern on the service between Archway and Potters Bar. This one is seen in Finchley when new.

◄ Riverside Bus branding was used by London United on 23 Leyland Olympians operated primarily on the 237 between Shepherds Bush and Sunbury Village. They were new in 1989 and had Cummins L10 engines and Leyland bodies built in the former National factory at Workington. The body was based on the design built by ECW between 1981 and 1987, but with detail differences. This is Hounslow in August 1995, after London United had been bought by its management.

▲ Photographed on the same day as the Olympian below left, a Westlink Optare Delta leaves Hounslow for Slough, a route which Westlink has just taken over from London Buslines. Westlink had been bought by its managers in 1994 and was then quickly sold to West Midlands Travel. It was bought by London United in September 1995. The Delta was based on a DAF SB220 chassis. London Buses bought 35 Deltas, nine of which were operated by Westlink and were of single-door layout.

▲ Eastern National's LRT operations were among those taken over by a new company, Thamesway, formed in 1990 after Badgerline bought Eastern National and split the company in two. This Dennis Dart with Plaxton Pointer body was new in 1996 and is seen in Church Street, Enfield, when just a few weeks old. FirstBus had come into being in 1995 with the merger of Badgerline and GRT. Initially the new group kept existing liveries but with fleetnames in a corporate style.

Capital Citybus was formed when the owners of Hong Kong Citybus purchased the LRT operations of Ensign Bus in 1991. Capital Citybus operated mainly in east and north-east London; this is Wood Green in 1996. The bus is a brand new Volvo Olympian with Northern Counties body. Capital Citybus was taken over by FirstBus in 1998.

◄ Armchair Passenger Transport was a respected coach operator based in Brentford. It diversified into bus operation, winning its first LRT contract in 1990. For this it bought a dozen stock Leyland Olympians with Alexander R-type bodies as seen here at Golders Green.

As it switched from running coaches to running buses Grey-Green found a novel way of making use of Volvo B10M coaches which it no longer needed: rebody them as buses. So in 1992 the company removed the Plaxton Paramount bodies from 16 B10Ms and had them rebodied by East Lancs. Seven were fitted with 49-seat single-deck bodies and nine with 73-seat double-deck bodies. Distinguishing features of the B10M double-deckers were the long wheelbase and the short rear overhang that was caused by fitting an 11m-long body on a chassis designed for a 12m-long coach.

▲ On most LRT contracts it was up to the operator to provide the buses, but where the contract was for a Routemaster route, LRT provided the vehicles. The happened on two contracts in 1993 involving Kentish Bus and BTS Coaches. The BTS Routemasters were painted poppy red, while those for Kentish Bus were in that company's standard maroon and cream. They were for service 19, Finsbury Park to Battersea Bridge. Route branding on the side precluded the application of adverts.

▲ First acquired CentreWest in 1997 and kept local identities such as Ealing Buses, as seen on this Marshall-bodied Dennis Dart SLF in Ealing. CentreWest was one of Marshall's biggest customers and by the end of 2000 was running over 250 Darts with this style of body, which was known as the Capital.

➤ The previous style of Marshall midibus body was a development of the body designed by Duple for the Dennis Dart, and subsequently built by Carlyle before being taken over by Marshall in 1991. Fifteen were built on MAN 11.220 chassis in 1996 for MTL London; this one is seen in Grays Inn Road.

◄ All the privatised London Buses subsidiaries retained the red livery which was synonymous with the buses of Britain's capital city, but most added details to differentiate their buses from those in other fleets. Metroline adopted a deep blue skirt and a striking fleetname, adding interest to the previously bland overall red of these buses. A 1980 Metrobus at the north end of Park Lane in 1996 illustrates the point.

The contract for the service between Kingston and Putney Bridge Station had been won by London & Country in 1980, and was still with the company when it became Arriva Croydon & North Surrey in 1998. The new Arriva company bought 13 DAF DB250s with Northern Counties Palatine II bodies for the route. Buses in Arriva's corporate colours were uncommon on London contracts.

Harris Bus was a short-lived London contractor, starting in 1997 then collapsing into receivership in 1999. This is Romford in 1998 when the future looked bright, and a smart Volvo Olympian is leaving for Ilford. It has an East Lancs Pyoneer body and was one of 35 delivered in 1997–98, indicative of the remarkable growth of the business.

▲ Travel West Midlands set up Travel London in 1998 to operate LTB contracted services. It purchased 21 Optare Excel integrals, one of which is seen in Victoria in 2000. The Excel had a Cummins engine and an Allison transmission.

▼ London's first low-floor double-deckers entered service in 1998. The early vehicles were DAF DB250s, Volvo B7TLs and, as here at Bank, Dennis Tridents. In 1999 First took 53 Tridents with Plaxton President bodies, shared between CentreWest and Capital Citybus, owner of this bus. The First logos flanking the destination display were illuminated at night. By the end of 1999 there were over 600 low-floor double-deckers running in London.

8
Britain's buses' brightest era

As the 1990s progressed, design house Best Impressions brought new elegance to bus liveries, combining relatively conventional layouts with striking colours and stylish fleetnames that hinted at the past while adding a modern flourish. Luton & District was among the beneficiaries. Bought by British Bus in 1994, it introduced a striking new livery the following year. It looked good even on this 17-year-old Bristol VRT, seen in Luton in 1997. By then known as LDT, the company used various local fleetnames such as Luton & Dunstable, as here. The VRT lasted another three years before withdrawal in 2000.

Historically, bus liveries were designed round the linear form of the vehicles they were applied to, typically consisting of a main colour and a secondary relief colour. Effectiveness relied on judicious choice of the colours, and finesse came with additional detailing such as a third colour for coach lining, which was often used to pick out the horizontal metal strapping that concealed the panel joints.

Applying all this could take many hours, but in the first part of the twentieth century labour was comparatively cheap, and the work required craft skills rather than design flair.

By the early 1980s the National Bus Company had abandoned nearly all this subtlety, applying a single colour (usually green or red) across nearly all its fleets, with just the concession of a white band between the decks of double-deckers. Sometimes single-deckers also featured the white band, but this was optional. Officially the objective of the change had been to establish an easily-recognised corporate identity, but given the blandness of the chosen livery, it is hard to dismiss the suspicion that cost reduction was seen as a useful by-product. To local travellers who might not have known what NBC buses looked like elsewhere, arguably the simplification of the livery was the *only* visible outcome.

The Scottish Bus Group had fared better in terms of its differentiated brands, retaining individual liveries for each constituent fleet, with just a standardised blue fleetname style indicating corporate ownership.

Council-owned fleets had also maintained a more traditional approach, but some of the PTEs had struggled to find liveries that respected the component businesses they were created from. Greater Manchester's orange and white (later orange, brown and white), admittedly a refreshing change from some of the traditional liveries it had replaced, was not to everyone's taste; Strathclyde's overall orange

▲ By 1980 the expensive practice of coach-lining was dying out in the bus world. This East Lancs-bodied Leyland Atlantean of Blackburn Transport, with its dark, heavy lining, gives a good idea of what was involved. Remarkably, Blackburn was using this former tramway livery as late as 1983, when the picture was taken, to replace the simpler 1970s livery seen on the bus behind it. Yet another, less complex livery would soon take its place.

▼ In 1980 thousands of NBC buses across England and Wales carried this same basic livery, with either red or green as the main colour. One thing that can be said for it is that it respected the lines of the bus. This Bristol Lodekka is a relatively rare long-wheelbase FL6B, with the raked front end used by ECW on rear-entrance models. New in 1962, it was still operating for Eastern Counties in Norwich after 18 years' service.

▲ Preston Borough Transport, like many municipal operators, updated its livery incrementally over the years. By September 1987 it was using the blue and cream design seen on the Leyland Atlantean on the left, but was also experimenting with slightly more adventurous ideas. The Atlantean in the centre has tri-tone blue stripes in place of the intermediate blue band, interrupted by a similar diagonal. The East Lancs bodywork also has then-modern features such as bonded glazing and asymmetric side windows at the front of the upper deck – derived from the bodybuilder's more dramatic coach front end, but arguably more elegant in this restrained form.

▼ Uniquely among privatised PTEs, Tyne & Wear's Busways retained a livery broadly dating back nearly 40 years, and even persevered with limited use of coach-lining to separate bands of colour. No racy diagonals here; the vivid cadmium yellow in use at the time of the sell-off endowed the fleet with a modern sparkle that probably gave the new owners the confidence to keep it more or less intact. This Scania N113 with Alexander PS bodywork is seen in Jesmond in June 1989, a few months after the company was sold to its management and employees.

▲ Eleven council bus operations had been absorbed into what became the Greater Manchester PTE, which replaced their various traditional liveries with an orange and white colour scheme that was high in impact, though arguably not in finesse. The version on its Metropolitans was non-standard, since the orange extended right up to the lower-deck windows. They were allocated to the Trans-Lancs Express service between Bolton, where this bus is seen in April 1981, and Stockport. Northern Counties-bodied Metrobuses, illustrated on page 33, were assigned to the route five years later.

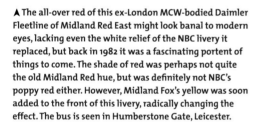

▲ The all-over red of this ex-London MCW-bodied Daimler Fleetline of Midland Red East might look banal to modern eyes, lacking even the white relief of the NBC livery it replaced, but back in 1982 it was a fascinating portent of things to come. The shade of red was perhaps not quite the old Midland Red hue, but was definitely not NBC's poppy red either. However, Midland Fox's yellow was soon added to the front of this livery, radically changing the effect. The bus is seen in Humberstone Gate, Leicester.

▲ When Midland Red East relaunched itself as Midland Fox in 1984 it broke with tradition in several ways, adopting a large fleetname and an even larger fox motif, and splashing yellow over the front of its red buses. The second colour stretched round to the sides, ending in a double-diagonal sweep. It was brash, but it certainly had impact. This ECW-bodied Daimler Fleetline, originally with Yorkshire Woollen District, was 13 years old when photographed in St Margaret's bus station, Leicester in May 1985.

was distinctly underwhelming; and few can have been impressed with South Yorkshire's unmemorable pale brown and cream.

Arguably Tyne & Wear PTE's yellow and white, based on the former Newcastle Corporation livery, was the most successful, and even retained the use of coach lining – though it may not have pleased the citizens of South Shields and Sunderland, whose municipal liveries it had replaced.

But the brave new world of privatisation and deregulation was felt to demand something different. A hint of what was possible came from the unlikely source of NBC, which introduced a new livery for coaches in the early 1980s, featuring a broad diagonal flash made up of thin horizontal stripes, the number, colour and thickness of which tended to vary from one fleet to another. This design, illustrated on page 19, was sometimes referred to as the Venetian blind livery.

As the wind of change blew through the bus industry, the more enlightened transport engineers and managers realised that if they wanted to make an impact with new bus liveries, they would probably need to go further than this – and they would require help.

NBC proved an unexpected facilitator here. After its years of uniformity, in its last throes it not only allowed member companies to develop new bus liveries, but even circulated a list of creative design houses that might be able to help them.

Not all companies took up this offer, but whether they did or not, one thing quickly became clear: broad diagonal colour swoops

of one sort or another were to be the order of the day over a large swathe of the industry.

Some operators applied the diagonals with little or no finesse, clearly anxious to keep costs to a minimum. Caldaire, with a range of fleets in the Yorkshire area, was among the worst offenders, simply applying a deep horizontal strip of solid colour with a token upsweep towards the front of the bus. However it did use rather elegant fleetnames, all in a standardised corporate style. ATL adopted a similar livery for some of its fleet, though without such an elegant fleetname.

There wasn't much more refinement in the yellow fronts applied to Midland Fox's underlying red, though at least there was an extra diagonal band of yellow where the colours abutted on the sides, suggesting a more considered approach.

Some early Stagecoach acquisitions also introduced a diagonal look, including CMS Carlislebus and United Counties.

The sheer brio of some of these new liveries helped to make the diagonal look work. The Badgerline colour scheme, featuring a vivid yellow and green, was one of the best examples. Even the bold two-tone blue and yellow of Kelvin Scottish had its admirers, though on traditional buses such as Routemasters the diagonal effect arguably looked particularly contrived.

The diagonal look achieved its most impressive form in a series of liveries developed by design house Hyphen Hayden. Northumbria Motor Services was probably the most memorable beneficiary;

▼ In search of a radical new look for its buses, privatisation-era operator North Western followed Northumbria by turning to design house Hyphen Hayden, and was rewarded with another striking design using diagonals that completely disregarded the shape of the bus. However, the design was simpler than Northumbria's, featuring all-over red apart from the dramatic blue frontal area with its grey and white borders. This Park Royal-bodied Leyland Atlantean had been new to Ribble in 1974, and is seen in Liverpool's Lord Street in June 1988.

▲ Probably the most radical new bus livery of the privatisation era was the remarkable red, white and grey colour scheme adopted by Northumbria in the mid-1980s, created by short-lived design house Hyphen Hayden. The bold diagonal colours paid no heed to the shape of the bus. The overall effect of Northumbria's striking livery is shown here in June 1989 in Newcastle's Osborne Road, Jesmond, on an ECW-bodied Leyland Olympian coach that had been new to London Country five years before.

diagonal bands of grey and red flared out across the front of the bus, seemingly taking no account of the underlying form. It shouldn't have worked, yet it did – helped by the subtle use of slim dividing bands of white, and by a stylised italic "N" logo that enhanced the effect.

Another company that received Hyphen Hayden's diagonal look was North Western. Again, there was considerable subtlety in the application, with abutting bands of white and blue marking the division between the principal blue and red colours. When Bee Line Buzz came into the same fold as North Western, a comparable diagonal livery was developed using Bee Line's existing yellow base colour. The same design company put up proposals for a diagonal look at Midland Red North, though this never came to fruition.

Northumbria stuck valiantly to its remarkable livery for more than ten years, but North Western and Bee Line Buzz switched to more traditional horizontal designs amid reports of difficulty in applying the diagonals consistently after repairs or during repainting.

Elsewhere, a more sympathetic approach to bus liveries gradually emerged. In place of arresting layouts, many operators put their faith in striking colours to make an impact – especially yellows and reds. Bristol City Line had led the way in 1985 with its remarkable harlequin confection of yellow, red and blue. The contrast with the

former NBC leaf green could hardly have been more emphatic. Now others followed – PMT, Midland Red North and Stevensons with their yellow and red, Derby with its yellow, red and blue, Eastern National with its yellow and green, Thamesway with yellow and maroon.

One of the most remarkable transformations was at the former South Yorkshire PTE, which adopted the Mainline identity in the late 1980s. Earlier it had given its bland beige and cream livery a little more impact by adding red to it, but now it introduced a vibrant new yellow and red colour scheme. Initially the second colour varied according to location, but soon the yellow and red look was pervasive – augmented by slim bands of silver.

Meanwhile, some privatised NBC companies revived liveries from their past, or at least approximations of them. Southdown reverted to apple green, Midland Red North and West Yorkshire to earlier shades of red, and East Yorkshire to dark blue , which was used selectively alongside a separate livery in new shade of red. Other new colour schemes such as Alder Valley South's green and yellow evoked the spirit of the past without slavishly recreating former liveries.

In the late 1980s one operator, SBG-owned Strathtay Scottish, went as far as to create a remarkable retro red and cream livery for the Routemasters it had acquired for Perth operations. This harked back to the colours used by Alexander from 1934, after it had taken

When Bee Line Buzz Company came into British Bus ownership it introduced a complex livery with a triangular frontal colour swatch in the same style as that of sister company North Western, as shown on the Atlantean on the opposite page. It had been new to Ribble in 1980, and is seen in Manchester's Piccadilly Gardens in August 1994.

◄ While Northumbria stuck with its diagonal livery until it was swept away by Arriva, North Western dropped its comparable version in the 1990s in favour of a much simpler linear design that respected the shape of the bus, but arguably lacked the panache of what had gone before. This Dennis Dominator has a bus body based on East Lancs' droop-fronted coach design. It was new to North Western in 1990, and is seen in Liverpool in August 1995.

over Perth Corporation's bus operations, until 1961. To underline the traditional message the Routemasters carried Perth City Transport fleetnames.

Stagecoach dropped the individual liveries of its member companies in the late 1980s, but the other emerging groups allowed local identities to persist for some years. Those of FirstBus subsidiaries sometimes lacked finesse, but there were exceptions; Yorkshire Rider, for instance, introduced increasingly stylish liveries using multi-tone green and cream.

As the 1990s unfolded, one particular design house, Best Impressions, made its mark on the industry, coming up with bold new designs such as Maidstone Borough Council's yellow and blue Boro'line identity. Later Best Impressions developed a series of designs that embodied the spirit of traditional bus operations in modern designs. Memorable examples included the yellow and blue of LDT (formerly Luton & District) and the green and cream of Maidstone & District. Sadly, both of these were soon abandoned in favour of Arriva's corporate look.

Yet those persistent diagonals wouldn't go away. The Go-Ahead group, for instance, initially adopted a bright but restrained red and white livery for its Northern General operations, enhanced by a strong new fleetname, but then in the 1990s it reinvented local operations such as Gateshead & District, giving them differentiated liveries, most of which featured a diagonal colour band.

Late in the 1990s Essex independent Harris Bus came up with a particularly elegant livery of pale green and blue, again by Best Impressions, in which the green and blue tapered into each other in a diagonal sweep near the front.

Among council-run fleets, Derby City Transport, Chesterfield Transport and Boro'line Maidstone were unusual for the period in adopting radically new fleet liveries. Most other local authority operators resisted the headlong rush to reinvent themselves visually, and merely updated their existing liveries with cautious incremental changes – Ipswich adding darker green, for instance, and Nottingham experimenting with the proportions of green and cream and altering the shade of green.

➤ The flamboyant yellow, red and blue livery adopted by Bristol Omnibus in the mid-1980s marked a radical break from NBC uniformity. As this July 1994 view of a Northern Counties-bodied Leyland Olympian shows, the diagonal element could be somewhat lost when partly obscured by advertisements, but the overall impact was undiminished. The bus is seen on part of the A38 in the heart of Bristol.

In the late 1980s Strathtay, a recent creation in the SBG fold, reinvented the long-defunct Perth City Transport identity to complement the reintroduction of open-platform buses in the area, and adopted this linear retro livery to go with it. The effect was remarkably convincing, although the rather low-key red and cream colour scheme itself was scarcely calculated to turn heads, especially when the newness wore off. This ex-London Routemaster was photographed in Perth in November 1989.

◄ Kelvin Scottish, the short-lived company created in 1985 from parts of Central, Eastern and Midland Scottish, adopted a bright two-tone blue and yellow livery. When newly applied, as seen on this ex-Midland Alexander-bodied Metrobus in August the following year, it was certainly striking; but the angular design could look awkward on the rounded form of the fleet's many Routemasters, and the idea of painting the front of a bus a different colour from the rest of it didn't sit well with purists.

However, several council fleets did change more significantly during the period. Grimsby Cleethorpes switched from pale brown and cream to a brighter orange and white. Merthyr Tydfil switched from brown and orange to blue and white. Southend replaced its muted blue and cream with a much brighter blue and white.

One council, Blackburn, had reverted by the early 1980s to something approaching its traditional green and cream tramway colour scheme, complete with coach lining. This replaced a more modern-looking livery of strong green, white and red that had been adopted in the 1970s.

Perhaps the Leicester fleet was the biggest surprise, featuring up to six different colour schemes in the period covered by this book (the exact number depends on what you consider a separate livery). Ironically, having replaced its mainly cream and maroon livery in

1984 with one of red, white and grey, in 1990 Leicester reintroduced a traditional 1940s-influenced maroon and cream livery, which would be considerably improved when it was adapted to conform to the short-lived but striking house style of its new parent GRT.

This was swept away when First introduced its nationwide corporate livery towards the end of the 1990s. A similar fate would befall all the former municipal, PTE, NBC and SBG fleets acquired by Arriva, First and Stagecoach.

Go-Ahead, however, kept the flag flying for differentiated liveries in its constituent fleets – a policy that broadly continued into the new century. But as 2000 dawned, variety in British bus liveries had been ratcheted back beyond anything NBC had imposed, and it would take a decade or more before individuality started to make a tentative impression again in some of those corporate fleets. ■

▲ Use of two or even three similar colours in close juxtaposition can endow a livery with depth and complexity. It worked well on the Preston bus shown on page 82, and was also effective in this late incarnation of Leicester's red and cream livery, seen in May 1997 on an East Lancs-bodied Dennis Dominator. The livery had been adapted to conform to the house style of GRT, which acquired Leicester Citybus 1994.

▲ Diagonal colour strips, largely a phenomenon of the 1980s, made a comeback ten years later in the livery of Travel West Midlands. This is one of 20 low-floor DAF-based Optare Spectras delivered in 1999, and is seen the following year on route 50, where they were concentrated before later moving to Wolverhampton. Despite its beguiling name, Druid's Heath was a mainly low-rise housing area in south Birmingham, developed by the council after the second world war to provide overspill capacity for the city's growing population.

9
The remarkable growth of Stagecoach

Stagecoach was primarily a long-distance coach operator when it took advantage of local bus deregulation to launch services in Glasgow in 1986 using a fleet of ex-London Transport AEC Routemasters with the Magicbus name. The Easterhouse Express on which this bus is operating used the M8 motorway to provide a faster journey, a rare instance of an open-platform bus running a local service on a motorway.

In 1980 Stagecoach started operations in Perth with two vehicles. In 2000 it had almost 7,500 buses and coaches in Britain, plus operations in Australia, New Zealand, Hong Kong, Portugal and the USA. This was a remarkable expansion and in many ways encapsulates the story of Britain's deregulated bus industry – unbridled competition slowly turning into settled local monopolies followed by expansion through acquisition and ending with a mature, stable and widely-respected business. It's a fable for the capitalist age. The driving force behind what would become one of Britain's best-known bus companies were brother and sister Brian Souter and Ann Gloag.

Coach deregulation fuelled the company's initial growth, with the introduction of a service from Dundee to London in 1980, which soon grew in to a network connecting Scotland's main cities with each other and Scotland with London. Ultimately, however, Stagecoach would withdraw from long-distance express coaching in 1989, selling that part of its business to National Express in order to focus on buses.

The company was already showing an interest in bus operation as early as 1986, taking advantage of local bus deregulation to introduce services in Glasgow. The buses

▲ Stagecoach introduced Routemasters to two of the NBC companies it acquired, United Counties and Cumberland Motor Services. This is Carlisle, where local services were branded as CMS Carlislebus. Stagecoach made full use of the London destination display.

▼ Most Olympians for Stagecoach were based on standard 9.5m chassis and had Alexander R-type bodies with 79 seats. Many of the English companies acquired by Stagecoach used the double curvature windscreen that had been specified by NBC on most of its ECW-bodied buses, and this became the standard on Stagecoach's Alexander R-types from 1991. Grimsby Cleethorpes received 15 in 1995.

it used, mostly ex-London Routemasters, were branded Magicbus and wore a variation of the white-with-stripes livery carried by Stagecoach coaches. The name, now written as Magic Bus, would reappear with an overall blue livery in the 1990s for cut-price services on busy routes in Glasgow, Manchester and Newcastle, designed to discourage potential competitors.

With the privatisation of NBC under way, in 1987 Stagecoach purchased four companies which between them were running over 700 vehicles – Hampshire Bus, Pilgrim Coaches, Cumberland and United Counties. Routemasters, which were operating successfully in Glasgow, were introduced to the Cumberland fleet in Carlisle and to United Counties in Bedford and Corby. In 1988 Stagecoach adopted the white-based livery carried by its express coaches for use on all its buses; like it or loathe it, this would be the group's standard livery until 2000.

More expansion quickly followed. In 1989 Stagecoach bought four former NBC companies from their management buy-out teams – East Midland, Ribble, Southdown and Hastings & District. Between them they added over 1,400 buses to the Stagecoach fleet, more than doubling its size. The acquisition of Ribble made Stagecoach the major operator in an area stretching from Preston to Carlisle.

There was expansion in the company's home territory, too. In 1989 Stagecoach purchased the assets of the short-lived Inverness Traction business from the receivers. Its Scottish operations would grow in 1991 with the purchase from SBG of Bluebird Buses and Fife Scottish, adding just over 500 vehicles to the fleet. To these it would add Western Scottish in 1994, buying the company from its managers.

After that, further expansion in Ayrshire spelled the end of the area's two old-established independent operators. The A1 co-operative was purchased in 1995, followed by AA Buses in 1997. Both operators' liveries were retained for some services.

More former NBC businesses joined Stagecoach in 1993, East Kent with 253 buses and Western Travel with 600. Through its ownership of East Kent, Hastings & District and Southdown, Stagecoach was now the principal operator on the south coast in an area stretching 150 miles from Margate to Portsmouth. Western Travel's operations included Cheltenham & Gloucester, Swindon & District, Midland Red South and – taking Stagecoach into Wales for the first time – Red & White. Red & White had been part of the troubled National Welsh business and in 1997 Stagecoach purchased Rhondda Buses, another remnant of that company.

Stagecoach's deregulation tactics were sometimes controversial. In Lancaster in 1993 and Darlington in 1994 it effectively forced the closure of the towns' municipal bus operations by registering competing service networks.

There were straightforward acquisitions involving local authority fleets. Grimsby Cleethorpes Transport was purchased in 1993, and was followed in 1994 by Cleveland Transit, Kingston-upon-Hull City Transport and Hartlepool Borough Transport.

The first major deal of 1994 was the purchase of Busways Travel Services, the former Tyne & Wear PTE bus operation, with a fleet of 600 vehicles. That was significant, but there was an even bigger deal in 1994, with the privatisation of London Buses. Stagecoach bought

◄ Stagecoach faced difficulties in Portsmouth. It bought both Portsmouth Citybus and Southdown in 1989, making it the major operator in the city. As with many of Stagecoach's acquisitions this displeased the Monopolies and Mergers Commission and as a result the former Citybus operations, by then part of Southdown Portsmouth, were sold to Transit Holdings in 1991. Although it looks much like the Atlanteans which Stagecoach acquired from Citybus, this bus in central Portsmouth in 1990 was in fact new to Grampian Regional Transport and was acquired by Stagecoach in 1989 with the East Midland business.

Vehicle policy

In the early days there was a measure of conservatism in the Stagecoach group's vehicle policy. Most major operators selected rear-engined chassis for single-deck buses on the basis that they offered easy two-step access, but Stagecoach opted for the mid-engined Volvo B10M, considering its reliability and low running costs a worthwhile benefit in exchange for an extra entrance step. Strict accessibility requirements for passengers with restricted mobility were still a long way in the future.

Most Stagecoach B10Ms had Alexander PS-type bodies. Indeed Alexander was from the start the group's main body supplier with R-types on Olympians, the AM Sprint on Mercedes midibuses, the Dash and ALX200 on Dennis Darts and Volvo B6s, and the ALX300 on MAN 18.220s. The latter replaced the Volvo B10M when the group switched to low-floor single-deckers in 1998. Volvo, which had been the group's biggest chassis supplier, also lost out in the move to low-floor double-deckers in 1999 when Stagecoach selected the Dennis Trident.

two London companies, East London and Selkent, adding a further 1,000 buses to its fleet to take the total to 6,000.

The expansion continued. In 1995 Cambus and Chesterfield Transport were acquired, followed in 1996 by former PTE operation GM Buses South, with 750 vehicles

Ribble was the major operator in Lancashire, and Stagecoach consolidated its position in East Lancashire in 1996 by buying two council-owned companies, Burnley & Pendle and neighbouring Hyndburn Transport in Accrington. In 1996–97 the operations of Transit Holdings in Devon, Oxford and London were acquired. This involved some 550 vehicles, most of them minibuses.

Stagecoach was always willing to innovate. In 1989 it put three tri-axle double-deckers in to service, the first new three-axle double-deck motorbuses in Britain for 50 years. They were based on Hong Kong-style Leyland Olympian chassis, and the most capacious of the trio, running in Glasgow, had 110 seats, a UK record.

Another approach to high carrying capacity was tried on some interurban services where Stagecoach introduced the UK's first articulated coaches. They were based on Volvo B10M chassis; 13 entered service in 1996–97. The artics had 71 seats – 20 more than a standard Plaxton-bodied B10M coach – and were initially operated by Fife Scottish, Ribble and East Midland.

The acquisition of Transit Holdings' Oxford operations in 1997 brought with it the Oxford Tube coach service to London. In 1999 the service was upgraded with a fleet of 27 MAN 24.350 three-axle double-deck coaches with 68-seat Jonckheere bodies.

In 2000 the white-with-stripes livery which had been the group standard since 1988 was replaced by a new, less brash, scheme with an off-white base and dark blue and red relief. ■

▲ The only new double-deckers delivered to Southdown in the two years in which it was owned by its management were 12 Volvo Citybuses with coach-seated Northern Counties bodies. They were delivered in the summer of 1989 in a livery which used Southdown's traditional shade of green. This Citybus in Portsmouth in 1990 gives no clue that it is owned by Stagecoach.

▼ East Midland was bought by Stagecoach in 1989 and among odd vehicles in the fleet were nine Leyland Tigers with 52-seat Alexander P-type bodies, an unusual choice for an NBC subsidiary. They were new in 1985, and by 1996 this one had acquired the corporate Stagecoach look. In common with a few other group subsidiaries, East Midland continued for a while to proclaim its identity using fleetnames in a non-standard style. The bus is passing through Sheffield on its way to Chesterfield, where East Midland was based.

▲ Grimsby Cleethorpes Transport took delivery of nine Dennis Lances in 1993. They were the only East Lancs-bodied Lances in the fleet of Stagecoach, which acquired the operator in November 1993. This is a 1997 view.

◀ The standard Stagecoach full-size single-decker from 1992 to 1998 was the Volvo B10M with Alexander PS-type body. Over 650 were purchased and the type was deployed in Stagecoach subsidiaries around the country. This Midland Red South example had 48 high-backed seats and was new in 1996. It is seen in Leamington Spa in 1998.

The growth of Stagecoach

Year	Company	Fleet size	Bought from
1987	Cumberland	230	NBC
	Hampshire Bus/Pilgrim Coaches	243	NBC (a)
	United Counties	250	NBC
1989	East Midland	300	NBC MBO
	Hastings & District	90	NBC MBO
	Portsmouth Citybus	114	Southampton Citybus (b)
	Ribble	800	NBC MBO
	Southdown	250	NBC MBO
1991	Fife Scottish	300	SBG
	Northern Scottish	209	SBG
1992	Alder Valley South (Aldershot area)	90	Q Drive
1993	East Kent	253	NBC MBO
	Grimsby Cleethorpes	111	Local authority
	Western Travel	600	NBC MBO
	Cheltenham & Gloucester		
	Midland Red South		
	Swindon & District		
	Red & White		
1994	Busways Travel Services	600	PTE MBO
	Cleveland Transit	141	Local authority MBO
	East London	590	London Buses
	Hartlepool Borough Transport	68	Local authority
	Kingston-upon-Hull City Transport	219	Cleveland Transit
	Selkent	390	London Buses
	Western Scottish	340	SBG MBO
1995	A1, Ardrossan	67	Owners
	Cambus/Milton Keynes Citybus	370	NBC MBO (c)
	Chesterfield Transport	134	Local authority MBO
1996	Burnley & Pendle	100	Local authority
	Devon General/Bayline	320	Transit Holdings
	GM Buses South	750	PTE MBO
	Hyndburn Transport	67	Local authority
1997	AA Buses, Troon	30	Dodds, Troon
	Docklands Transit	48	Transit Holdings
	Rhondda Buses	100	Owners
	Thames Transit	180	Transit Holdings
1998	Sheffield Supertram	-	-
2000	Heysham Travel	30	MTL

● Only fleets of 25 or more vehicles are included. There were other, smaller, acquisitions.

● MBO – management buy-out.

(a) Pilgrim Coaches closed 1987.

(b) Portsmouth Citybus sold 1991.

(c) Milton Keynes Citybus sold 1997.

▲ East Kent was another 1993 acquisition by Stagecoach. As a former NBC subsidiary it had the typical mix of Leyland Nationals and Bristol VRTs, but unusually the latter included some with angular full-height bodywork by Willowbrook. NBC had taken 57 Willowbrook-bodied VRTs in 1978 with 28 going to East Kent and 29 to Northern General. The privatised East Kent company adopted a livery which recalled that used before NBC's poppy red, as seen in Canterbury bus station in 1994.

➤ Cleveland Transit and the associated Kingston-upon-Hull City Transport business were bought by Stagecoach in 1994. Hull's buses were by then in a livery based on that used by Cleveland, but with blue in place of Cleveland's green. Stagecoach fleetnames are carried on this 1989 East Lancs-bodied Dennis Dominator in 1996.

In the 1990s Stagecoach was arguably the big group that took the greatest care of its fleet. This is Bath in 1998, when the ECW-bodied Bristol VRT from the Cheltenham & Gloucester fleet was an impressive 23 years old.

▼ Between 1992 and its acquisition by Stagecoach in 1995 Cambus bought 22 Optare MetroRiders. This was the first, and it is seen in Cambridge in 1998. The Cowley Road destination would work equally well in Cambridge's rival university city, Oxford.

▲ Magic Bus services were introduced by Stagecoach in Manchester and Glasgow in the late 1990s offering lower fares and generally operated by older vehicles. There was no indication that the buses were owned by Stagecoach, although the fleet number in the Stagecoach Manchester series might have been a clue for observant passengers. In 1998 the Manchester Magic Bus fleet included this 14-year-old Leyland Olympian which had been acquired with the business of GM Buses South in 1996.

The buses operated by Stagecoach in London were red with white corporate fleetnames – except on Routemasters, where the fleetname was in gold, a sympathetic choice in keeping with the vehicles' heritage. There is also a small Routemaster name above the fleetnumber, a feature used on these buses back in their early years. A 30ft-long RML heads east in Oxford Street in 1995. The bus was almost 30 years old

◄ Thames Transit, with 180 buses, was Stagecoach's last major acquisition in the 1990s. The Oxford-based business was purchased in 1997. Thames Transit was running 62 Dennis Darts with Plaxton Pointer bodies when Stagecoach took over. One pulls out of the Queen Street pedestrian zone in 1996 heading for Rose Hill on the southern edge of the city.

▼ When Stagecoach placed bulk orders for full-size low-floor buses from 1998 the orders went not to Volvo, but to German manufacturer MAN, at that time something of a fringe supplier as far as British bus operators were concerned. An initial order for 150 was followed by further orders and by the end of 2000 Stagecoach was running over 300 MAN 18.220s with 42-seat Alexander ALX300 bodies. Most carried LoLiner branding, as on this Stagecoach Busways vehicle in Newcastle.

➤ Stagecoach had standardised on Volvo B10M single-deckers during the 1990s, so observers might reasonably have expected it to stick with Volvo when it switched to the new generation of low-floor models. It did take five Volvo B10BLEs with attractive Northern Counties bodies in 1997 and these were initially operated by Stagecoach Manchester. At a time when low-floor buses were still something of a novelty it's noteworthy that this bus's livery doesn't make any mention of ease of access.

The sometimes tortuous plans of London Transport have at various times in the organisation's history seen relatively good buses being withdrawn prematurely only to be snapped up by other operators.

LT considered its DMS-class Daimler Fleetlines a failure, and started selling them off when some were just seven years old, roughly half way through their design life.

Many found a future elsewhere, notably with the West Midlands PTE, which bought 80, and subsidiaries of the National Bus Company, which took over 100. Other operators bought smaller numbers. These included the Scottish Bus Group and the Greater Manchester PTE, as well as a few municipals and independent operators. In the mid 1980s some small operators used these redundant Fleetlines on tendered services in London. Did anyone at London Buses, as the operation was now known, notice the irony?

Then came the most unlikely bus type to find a new lease of life – the Routemaster. Could anybody at London Buses really believe it when they found that these outdated vehicles might be worth more than their scrap value? But they were, and in 1986–87 operators around the country bought Routemasters as they looked for ways to win customers in deregulated Britain. SBG was the biggest buyer, with 168, most of which were operated in Glasgow. Other well-known users included Blackpool Transport, Burnley & Pendle, Greater Manchester Buses, Stagecoach and Southend Transport.

London Buses started reducing its fleet as it lost routes to new operators under the tendering regime, and at that point more modern types also found a new lease of life elsewhere. Metrobuses, Titans and Leyland Nationals were bought by a range of mainly small operators in the late 1980s and early 1990s.

After London Buses was privatised some of the large national groups that had purchased a London company would transfer redundant vehicles to their fleets elsewhere, including Stagecoach with Titans and Arriva with Metrobuses.

▲ Of all the London buses that operated elsewhere in Britain, few attracted as much attention as the Routemaster. They were bought by three Scottish Bus Group companies in the mid 1980s, Clydeside, Strathtay and, as seen here in Glasgow in 1986, Kelvin.

➤ The saga of London Transport's premature Fleetline disposals was a sorry tale; most of the 2,646 buses that made up LT's DMS and DM class had short lives in the capital. This bus entered service in 1975 and was withdrawn in 1982 on the expiry of its initial seven-year Certificate of Fitness. In 1986 it was bought by Sampsons of Cheshunt and used on a London Regional Transport contracted service in the Enfield area.

◀ NBC subsidiaries bought over 100 redundant London Fleetlines. This is another 1975 bus which was sold by LT in 1983. Between 1983 and 1986 it was operated by South Wales Transport – this is Swansea in 1984. It was then sold to Wilts & Dorset, where it ran until 1991.

◀ The purchase of 80 second-hand buses was an unprecedented move by the West Midlands PTE. In 1980 it was running around 1,900 Fleetlines. Like all British bus operators it was faced with the phasing out of the government's new bus grant. So it reduced its intake of new buses and instead seized the opportunity to stock up with 80 ex-London Fleetlines. These were supplied by Ensign Bus, which removed the centre exit before repainting them and sending them to the PTE. A seven-year-old Fleetline is seen in Solihull in the summer of 1980. It operated for West Midlands until 1985.

ROUTEMASTERS FOR SALE

LONDON BUSES OFFERS FOR SALE REFURBISHED 64 SEAT ROUTEMASTER BUSES DESIGNED FOR USE IN HIGH DENSITY URBAN AREAS. REALISTIC PRICES COUPLED WITH ECONOMIC OPERATING COSTS AND THE ABILITY TO BEAT COMPETITORS SERVICES ON JOURNEY TIMES CAN OFFSET THE HIGHER COST OF CREW OPERATION. THE LIGHTWEIGHT INTEGRAL ALLOY BODY GIVING A WEIGHT OF ONLY 7.5 TONNES GIVES EXCEPTIONAL FUEL CONSUMPTION IN URBAN AREAS. VEHICLES ARE OFFERED WITH FFD CERTIFICATE AND REPAINTED INTERNALLY AND EXTERNALLY FROM **£7000 + VAT.** OPEN TOP CONVERSIONS SUBJECT TO QUOTATION. COMMERCIAL MOTOR ROADTEST REPORT IN JULY 12, 1986 ISSUE.

ENQUIRIES TO: SALES MANAGER
LONDON BUSES LTD
566 CHISWICK HIGH ROAD
LONDON W4 5RR
TELEPHONE: 01-994 9494

AD0858M

COMMERCIAL MOTOR w-e August 2, 1986

▲ Facing growing competition on the busy Wilmslow Road corridor GM Buses bought ten Routemasters in 1988. They terminated in Piccadilly Gardens, Manchester's main bus station, and carried Piccadilly Line branding. They were withdrawn in 1990.

▲ Low winter sun casts dappled shadows on two Routemasters running for Southend Transport in December 1988. Unlike some operators, Southend made full use of the ample rear destination display. Routemaster operation ended in 1993 after the business was bought by British Bus.

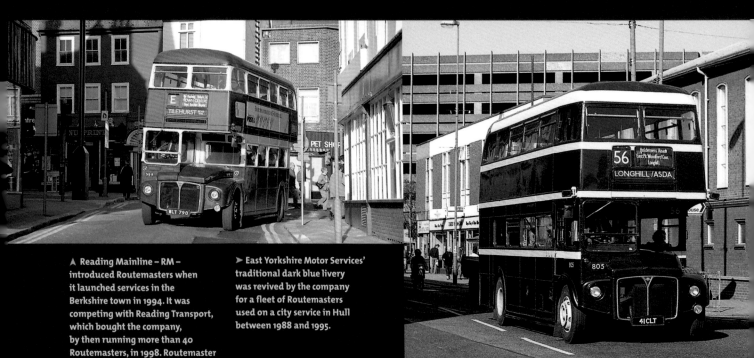

▲ Reading Mainline – RM – introduced Routemasters when it launched services in the Berkshire town in 1994. It was competing with Reading Transport, which bought the company, by then running more than 40 Routemasters, in 1998. Routemaster operation ended in 2000.

➤ East Yorkshire Motor Services' traditional dark blue livery was revived by the company for a fleet of Routemasters used on a city service in Hull between 1988 and 1995.

▶ In the late 1990s Stagecoach transferred elderly Titans from its London operations to fleets elsewhere in the country. New in 1982, this bus was moved to Middlesbrough in 1998 where it joined the Stagecoach Transit fleet.

▲ Merseyside Transport bought over 200 Leyland Titans from London Buses between 1992 and 1994, making it the biggest operator of Leyland's integral bus outside London. This is Hood Street, Liverpool, in 1995 with a 1980 Titan.

Routemasters were introduced to Blackpool in 1986 and operated until 1996. They were run by Blackpool Transport in a distinctive red and white livery with elaborate and finely detailed coach lining.

10
First, Britain's biggest bus group

First 🍋

First invested heavily in new vehicles, and this Volvo
Olympian was part of an order for 78 with Alexander
Royale bodies delivered in 1998. Despite being 10.3m
long they had just 72 seats, as First tried to improve
the comfort of its vehicles. First Yorkshire got 56 of the
Royales with the remainder going to Scotland to the
associated Midland Bluebird and Lowland fleets. A
First Yorkshire bus passes Leeds Town Hall in 1999.

When Badgerline and GRT merged to create FirstBus in 1995 the name was more an aspiration than a statement of fact. FirstBus may have had an impressive 5,600 buses and coaches but it was in reality SecondBus to Stagecoach, whose fleet numbered around 6,000.

The original Badgerline business covered part of what had been the Bristol Omnibus Company's country area. It was created in 1986 and was privatised in a management-led employee buy-out later that year, headed by managing director Trevor Smallwood.

It soon started expanding and by 1994 had a significant portfolio of former NBC companies including Eastern National and Thamesway, Western National, Midland Red West, Bristol Omnibus, South Wales Transport and PMT. Its biggest single expansion, in 1994, came with the purchase of Yorkshire Rider, the former West Yorkshire PTE bus operation, with 1,100 buses. At this point Badgerline had 4,000 vehicles.

GRT was founded on a management-led employee buy-out of Grampian Regional Transport in 1989 with Moir Lockhead at the helm. It, too, was quick to expand and in 1994 owned three former SBG fleets, Midland, Eastern and Lowland; two English municipals, Northampton Transport and Leicester City Bus; and one former NBC company, Eastern Counties. This gave it a fleet of 1,600 vehicles, of which around 1,100 were in Scotland.

While it may have been the smaller partner, GRT emerged as the dominant force in FirstBus. Acquisitions in the second half of the 1990s saw FirstBus overtake Stagecoach to become truly first, at least in terms of fleet size. At the end of 1996 FirstBus had 8,000 vehicles, putting it ahead of Stagecoach with 7,100.

The companies that became part of First included south coast operators People's Provincial, Portsmouth Transit (successor to Portsmouth City Transport) and Southampton City Bus, giving First

▲ The smaller of the two partners in FirstBus was GRT, but it quickly emerged as the dominant force. GRT had its roots in Grampian Regional Transport, whose core business was running local buses in Aberdeen. Its fleet was made up mainly of Alexander-bodied Leyland double-deckers, the newest being Olympians as seen here in the city's main thoroughfare, Union Street, in 1994.

▼ Badgerline was the bigger of the FirstBus partners. It had adopted this livery while still part of NBC. Not all privatised NBC companies remained loyal to the group's principal chassis supplier, Leyland, and the independent Badgerline's first new vehicles in 1987 were 40 Volvos. These included 12 Citybuses with Alexander R-type bodies, one of which is seen when new in Weston-super-Mare. Stylised badgers flank the destination display.

a substantial urban presence in an area served largely by Stagecoach. Further west it would add Southern National and North Devon Red Bus in 1999. First already owned the neighbouring Western National company, and thus became the main operator in an area stretching from Bristol to Land's End.

On the east coast it acquired Great Yarmouth Transport, which fitted in with Eastern Counties. Its biggest acquisitions, both coming in 1996, were two former PTE operations, GM Buses North in Manchester with 950 buses and SB Holdings in Glasgow, with 1,250. The latter included not just the ex-PTE Strathclyde Buses fleet but also Kelvin Central, a one-time SBG operation acquired by SB Holdings in 1994. This established First as the major operator in central Scotland in an area stretching from Berwick on the east coast, through the Lothians, Lanarkshire, Glasgow and Dumbartonshire to Balfron in mid-Stirlingshire.

First was the principal operator in West Yorkshire through its ownership of Yorkshire Rider. In 1998 it became the main operator in neighbouring South Yorkshire when it acquired Mainline which, like Yorkshire Rider, was originally PTE-owned.

First had a small presence in London through its Thamesway subsidiary but in 1997 it expanded in the capital with the purchase of CentreWest. This brought with it part of the former NBC Alder Valley North business, latterly known as the Bee Line Bus Co. To this it would add Capital Citybus in 1998.

Vehicle policy

In the early 1990s GRT had focused on vehicle quality, buying single-deck buses with air-conditioning and double-glazing. These were supplied by Mercedes-Benz and Scania. It experimented with an articulated Mercedes-Benz, the first (and last) articulated bus to be bodied by Alexander. GRT viewed single-deckers as being more attractive to its passengers and bought no new double-deckers.

The Badgerline group bought double-deckers for specific operations, for instance Volvo Olympians for Bristol, but also tended to favour single-deckers, most commonly Dennis Darts and Lances, although it did also have a large fleet of Leyland Lynxes.

As FirstBus, the combined group ordered Olympians for its double-deck requirements, mostly with stylish Alexander Royale bodies, an indication of its pursuit of quality. Single-deckers were mainly Dennis Darts and Wright-bodied Scanias and Volvos. In 1999 the group introduced 40 articulated Volvos to services in Glasgow, Leeds and Manchester, and a further 30 followed in 2000. There was some interest in alternative fuels in the late 1990s and First carried out small scale evaluations of CNG, LPG and battery-electric buses.

◄ GRT had a corporate identity which respected local traditions. The cream base colour on this Northampton Transport bus is the same as on the Grampian vehicle illustrated on page 101, but relieved with red – the previous colour of Northampton's buses – rather than green. Northampton standardised on Volvo Citybuses from 1986 and by 1992 was running 32. It also had five mechanically-similar B10M single-deckers, four of which had relatively rare Duple 300 bus bodies with high-backed seats. This was the first, new in 1988 and seen entering the town's bus station in 1995.

◄ In 1993 GRT bought both the Northampton and Leicester municipal fleets, located some 40 miles apart. Their proximity to one another made it easy for the fleets to loan vehicles to each other, and here a Leicester Dennis Dominator is operating on hire to Northampton Transport in 1995. This livery had been introduced by Leicester in 1990 and was replaced by a red-based livery in GRT corporate style, as shown on the opposite page. The vast edifice in the background housed Greyfriars Bus Station, a dismal windswept cavern.

▼ Badgerline bought large numbers of Dennis Lances with Plaxton Verde bodies. The biggest user was Yorkshire Rider, which received 48 in 1995 followed by another 30 in 1996. This one is in Huddersfield in 1999. The two-tone green and cream livery had been introduced by Badgerline.

▲ In 1995 FirstBus divided Yorkshire Rider into four separate operating units. Services in Leeds were operated by Leeds City Link in this bright colour scheme which was a complete break with the city's tradition of green buses. The bus is one of 25 MCW Metrobus IIs delivered in 1988. It was photographed in 1999.

➤ Two-tone blue was used for the Bradford Traveller fleet, acknowledging the livery once worn by the city's municipal buses. It is seen on a 1990 Northern Counties-bodied Leyland Olympian.

Initially FirstBus subsidiaries retained their own liveries but with fleetnames in a corporate First style. Then in 1997 the group introduced a white, magenta and blue corporate livery – although in the early days its widespread use was constrained by a group policy which dictated that it should only be applied to new buses featuring the group's innovative colour co-ordinated interior. By contrast, Stagecoach and then Arriva were unequivocal in their adoption of corporate colours, which were applied to virtually every bus outside London.

The major flaw in First's approach was that buses typically have a 15-year life, which meant that it would be around 2012 before all First's buses were in corporate colours. First had a rethink and in 2001 would adopt a modified version of its new livery for use on older buses.

By 2000 First was running 10,000 vehicles in Britain, making it the biggest British bus operator well ahead of Stagecoach and Arriva, each with around 7,500. ■

▼ Small three-axle buses were rare and the most successful was the Talbot Pullman. Midland Red West took seven in 1990 and this one is operating in Worcester in 1996, the year in which the last of them were withdrawn. The Pullman was developed from the front-wheel-drive Talbot Express van and with its small wheels offered a lower floor than any of its rivals.

▲ GM Buses North was acquired by FirstBus in 1996. For a time the fleet was painted overall orange, as illustrated by a 1995 Volvo B10B with 50-seat Wright Endurance body in central Manchester.

◄ First introduced its new corporate look in 1997, with a livery soon nicknamed Barbie because the band of magenta relief resembled the colour associated with the doll of the same name produced by US toy manufacturer Mattel. This Provincial Dennis Dart SLF with 40-seat Plaxton Pointer body is seen in Portsmouth in 1998 when the bright new livery was still something of a novelty.

With the purchase of CentreWest in 1997 First became a Routemaster operator. A First Gold Arrow RML makes its way along Queen Victoria Street on its route from Liverpool Street Station to Westbourne Park in 1999, when the company was running just under 50 Routemasters.

◄ Southampton Citybus experimented with compressed natural gas in the 1990s, first converting six existing diesel-engined Dennis Darts to CNG and then in 1996 buying ten new CNG-powered Darts including this example, photographed in 1998. The gas was stored in tanks on the roof. The trial was continued by First after it bought Citybus in 1997.

The growth of FirstBus

Year	Company	Fleet size	Bought from
Badgerline			
1986	Badgerline	400	NBC
1987	Western National	300	NBC (a)
1988	Midland Red West	425	NBC MBO
	Bristol City Line	360	NBC MBO
1990	South Wales Transport	350	NBC MBO
	Eastern National	470	NBC MBO (b)
	Wessex Coaches	33	NBC MBO
1994	PMT	500	NBC MBO
	Yorkshire Rider	1,100	PTE MBO
1995	*merged with GRT*		
GRT			
1989	Grampian Transport	210	Local authority
1990	Midland Scottish	280	SBG
1993	Northampton	56	Local authority
	Leicester	220	Local authority
1994	Eastern Counties	370	NBC MBO
	Eastern Scottish	371	SBG MBO
	Lowland Omnibuses	159	SBG MBO
1995	*merged with Badgerline*		

Year	Company	Fleet size	Bought from
First			
1995	Badgerline	4,000	-
	GRT	1,600	-
	Provincial	155	NBC employee buy-out
1996	GM Buses North	950	PTE MBO
	Portsmouth Transit	145	Transit Holdings
	SB Holdings	1,250	PTE MBO
	Strathclyde Buses		
	Kelvin Central Buses		
	Great Yarmouth Transport	46	Local authority
1997	CentreWest London Buses	500	London Buses MBO
	Bee Line Bus Co		
	London Buslines		
	Southampton Citybus	140	Local authority MBO
1998	Mainline	800	PTE MBO
	Capital Citybus	300	Management
	Timeline, Manchester	51	Management (c)
1999	Cawlett	400	NBC MBO
	North Devon Red Bus		
	Southern National		
	Biss Bros/Airport Coaches	25	Lynton Travel
	Davies, Pencader	38	Receivers

● Only acquired fleets of 25 or more vehicles are included. There were other, smaller, acquisitions.

● MBO – management buy-out.

(a) Bought jointly with Plympton Coachlines; Badgerline assumed total control in 1988.

(b) Eastern National was divided in 1990, with south Essex depots being taken over by a new Thamesway subsidiary.

(c) First acquired part of Timeline's Manchester area business, with the remainder being acquired by Arriva, along with 20 buses.

The Dennis Dart was without question the best-selling urban bus in the last twenty years of the 20th century. But Dennis's earlier forays in to urban single-deck buses were not quite so impressive.

First was the Dominator, 36 of which were bodied as single-deckers between 1978 and 1980. The single-deck Dominator was replaced by the Falcon which, for bus use, had a horizontal Gardner engine rather than the vertical unit of the Dominator. This did rather better, with 103 Falcon buses being built between 1981 and 1993. In addition six were bodied as double-deckers and ten were built as coaches for the National Bus Company. These two variants had V engines, a Mercedes V6 in the double-deckers and a Perkins V8 in the coaches.

The Lance was somewhat more successful. It was built between 1991 and 1997 for the home market, and a final batch of 20 was built for export to Singapore in 2000. The Lance was quite a different beast from the Falcon. It was lighter and cheaper, and in place of the 10.45-litre Gardner 6HLXB which powered the Falcon there was an 8.3-litre Cummins C-series. From 1993 the Lance was the standard single-decker for the Badgerline Group, and was supplied to former Badgerline

companies in FirstBus until 1997. Most of Badgerline's 182 Lances had Plaxton Verde bodies. The Go-Ahead Group took 34 with Optare Sigma bodies for its Gateshead and Brighton subsidiaries. Caldaire had 30 Alexander-bodied Lances in Yorkshire, while British Bus had 35 in its Clydeside, North Western and London & Country fleets.

London Buses was the next biggest user after the Badgerline Group, buying 59 Lances with bodies by Alexander, Northern Counties and Plaxton. London Buses also influenced the development of a new Lance, the SLF, which had independent front suspension and provided a step-free entrance. This made boarding easier for people with impaired mobility and opened up services to parents with children in baby buggies.

The Lance SLF, like most step-free buses in Britain, was essentially a low-entry vehicle with an internal step ahead of the rear axle, rather than a European-style low-floor model with a step-free gangway running the full length of the bus. The advantage of the approach used by Dennis was that the drivetrain was simpler and cheaper than on a full low-floor chassis. While just 105 Lance SLF chassis were built in 1994–95, the model paved the way for the Dart SLF which was the most successful low-entry model of its time.

The Lance SLFs were bodied by two builders, Wright and Berkhof. The biggest user was London with 38, followed by Speedlink Airport Services with 30 which it operated at Heathrow Airport. The others were run in small numbers by a variety of operators wanting to evaluate the benefits of easy-access buses.

There was one final Lance development: a double-decker. Sales of the double-deck Dominator in Britain had peaked as early as 1982. In 1992 and 1993 deliveries were in single figures. The Dominator was an old design, and building a specialised chassis in small numbers was inefficient and expensive. The solution was to use the short-wheelbase Lance with modified suspension and a shorter rear overhang. The Lance double-decker was launched at Coach & Bus 95, the industry's biennial trade exhibition. However there was a clear sign at the exhibition that changes were coming to double-deck bus design, with DAF exhibiting a low-floor chassis.

In early 1996 the Lance name was dropped for the double-decker, which became the Arrow – although not before a few had been delivered with Lance badges. The model had a short life, with just 73 having been built when production ended in 1998. The biggest user was Capital Citybus with 54. However the low-floor Trident which succeeded it would for a time be Britain's best-selling double-decker.

A total of 589 Lances, Lance SLFs and Arrows were built for

⬆ Before the introduction of the Lance, the Gardner-engined Falcon was the main Dennis single-deck model aimed at urban bus operators. Just over 100 were built between 1981 and 1993. Grimsby Cleethorpes took four

➤ The 1991 Lance was lighter than the Falcon and was powered by an in-line 8.3-litre Cummins C-series engine in place of the Falcon's transverse 10.45-litre Gardner. The last Lances to enter service in Britain were 13 for First Eastern National in early 1997. They had 49-seat Northern Counties Paladin bodies, as seen in Colchester in 1998.

▼ The Lance was developed as a double-decker, with Capital Citybus being the main buyer. This is a 1998 bus with East Lancs Pyoneer body, photographed in 1999 after First had purchased Capital Citybus. All the operator's Arrows would be transferred to other First companies in the early 2000s.

▲ The ultimate version of the Lance was the SLF, one of the first low-floor buses to be built in Britain. London took 38 in 1994 with Wright Pathfinder bodies. London United had the first ten.

11
Arriva: a new name in buses

Many British Bus subsidiaries used bright
liveries. These included Derby City Transport
as shown by a brand new Northern Counties-bodied
Volvo Olympian in the summer of 1996. Derby had two of
these Olympians out of a batch of 20 ordered by British Bus.
With the new look came a new City Rider fleetname.

The companies at the core of what in 1997 became Arriva Passenger Services had previously been part of British Bus, and before that, Drawlane. So it was very much a child of deregulation and privatisation. But its bus industry roots actually go back to 1980, the year when the Sunderland-based Cowie car dealing group bought London coach operator Grey-Green. Under Cowie ownership Grey-Green would abandon coaching and re-invent itself as a bus operator running services under contract to London Regional Transport.

Put Cowie at the back of your mind, and fast forward to 1987. That was when Drawlane, a new name in the bus world, bought Shamrock & Rambler in Bournemouth, its first acquisition as part of the privatisation of NBC. Drawlane had been formed by businessman Ray McEnhill who ran Endless Holdings, a multi-faceted organisation which took its name from Endless Street in Salisbury, where the company was based.

Three more NBC companies were acquired in 1988, London Country South West, Midland Red North and North Western. This gave Drawlane a fleet of almost 1,100 buses and coaches. Shamrock & Rambler was quickly closed, but the other three companies thrived.

An unusual move in this era was Drawlane's purchase of East Lancashire Coachbuilders, based in Blackburn. It had been owned by the John Brown engineering group, and was acquired in 1988. East Lancs wasn't big enough to meet all of Drawlane's growing requirements for new vehicles but it became a regular supplier of bodies, often on Dennis chassis that included Darts, Dominators and Falcons.

Soon Drawlane was growing. It became established in Manchester in 1989 by buying the Frontrunner North West and Bee Line Buzz operations from Stagecoach, along with some Ribble

▲ This is the livery used by former NBC subsidiary Luton & District in the late 1980s. On the left is an Alexander-bodied Leyland Olympian, one of 12 bought in 1988 which were the privatised company's first new double-deckers. A further 13 followed in 1989. On the right is a typical NBC VRT, new to Luton & District predecessor United Counties in 1977. Following its acquisition by British Bus in 1994, Luton & District replaced this livery with a colourful new look, as shown on page 80.

▼ London Country South East was transformed into Kentish Bus in 1987, and adopted this livery to replace the NBC leaf green used by LCSE. The bus is a typical London Country Leyland Atlantean with 73-seat Roe body from a batch of 30 which entered service in the winter of 1979–80. This is Gravesend in 1988.

services. In the same year it bought Crosville and Midland Fox. Crosville had been owned by the short-lived ATL organisation while Midland Fox had been a management buy-out from NBC.

The latter purchase gave it two of the four Midland Red companies, while the former meant it briefly had significant operations around Liverpool with Crosville to the south and North Western to the north. Parts of Crosville were soon taken over by other Drawlane companies – North Western, Bee Line and Midland Fox – leaving Crosville with 155 buses in Merseyside, Wirral and Chester. This operation was sold to PMT in 1990, marking the disappearance of the long-standing Crosville name from north-west England. However, while it gave up on what might be described as the English Crosville business, in 1992 Drawlane acquired Crosville Wales from National Express.

In 1989 London Country South West was given a new look designed by Best Impressions, and started trading as London & Country. In 1990 it expanded with the acquisition of Q Drive's Alder Valley operations in and around Guildford. This involved 50 buses and was operated as Guildford & West Surrey using a livery similar to that of London & Country.

There were structural changes in the Drawlane organisation in 1992 out of which emerged British Bus. In 1993 the new company acquired two council-owned bus businesses in Essex, at Colchester and Southend. There was expansion elsewhere, with North Western buying Liverline, set up by former Merseyside PTE employees in 1988 and running 51 buses.

This was followed in 1994 by Stevensons of Uttoxeter and Luton & District. The latter had a stake in Derby City Transport and

Cowie subsidiary Grey-Green bought 30 Alexander-bodied Volvo Citybuses in 1988 for LRT route 24 between Hampstead Heath and Pimlico. In 1989 this bus has strayed on to another LRT service. The Citybus was undeniably a reliable vehicle, but its high floor was a drawback on busy urban routes.

In 1995 Midland Red North, whose buses were overall dark red, adopted a brighter livery. This is Cannock in 1996 and the bus is a former London Country Leyland Tiger. When new in 1982 it was a 49-seat ECW-bodied Green Line coach. It was one of a number transferred to Midland Red North in 1990 and rebodied by East Lancs as 51-seat buses.

Clydeside 2000, and by the end of the year these, too, were part of British Bus. At the same time it took over Proudmutual, which owned Northumbria, Moor Dale and Kentish Bus. In just 12 months the British Bus fleet doubled from 2,000 to 4,000 vehicles.

The expansion continued in 1995 with the purchase of Caldaire, which ran 400 buses. These were operated by West Riding, Yorkshire Woollen, Selby & District and South Yorkshire Transport. Maidstone & District, with 300 buses, also entered the British Bus fold in 1995.

In 1994 Cowie re-enters the story with the purchase of London Buses' Leaside subsidiary, followed in 1995 by South London. Add the Grey-Green fleet, which was running London tendered services, and Cowie was the capital's biggest bus operator with over 1,000 vehicles. It expanded in 1996 with the acquisition of County Bus & Coach and Westcourt from West Midlands Travel. Westcourt owned United, TMS, and Tees & District.

But the big news in 1996 was the takeover of British Bus by Cowie. British Bus ran 5,200 vehicles while Cowie had just 1,200. That makes it look like a David versus Goliath story, but in fact Cowie with its motor trade interests was a much bigger business than British Bus.

One of the effects of the 1996 expansion was to re-unite Northumbria with United, and to give Cowie control of most of what had been London Country Bus Services. County Bus & Coach had

been a major part of London Country North East. It joined LCSW, which had been in Drawlane ownership since 1988; LCNW, which had been acquired by British Bus with Luton & District in 1994; and LCSE, now re-named Kentish Bus, which came with Proudmutual, also in 1994.

The Cowie takeover saw British Bus sever its relationship with East Lancs, which was sold to a group of Jersey-based investors. In 1988 Cowie had bought the Hughes DAF coach dealership in Cleckheaton, near Huddersfield, in an expansion of its motor trade interests. DAF chassis would feature in the group's future deliveries; indeed, by 2000 there were over 200 DAFs in its London fleets alone.

Cowie had kept a low profile in the bus industry, but the British Bus acquisition in 1996 made it the third largest bus operator in Britain after FirstBus and Stagecoach. A year later it decided to introduce branding that reflected the scale of its activities. In came the Arriva name and a corporate livery for its bus business, out went the local identities of its many subsidiaries. While British Bus never had a corporate identity, a number of its fleets had used strong, bright, colours. North Western and Derby, for example, were red, yellow and blue, Midland Red North was red and yellow while LDT (Luton & District as was) used blue and yellow. All these liveries now disappeared.

◄ When the West Yorkshire PTE set up its arm's length Yorkshire Rider company it disposed of a number of modern buses, including some five-year-old Alexander-bodied MCW Metrobuses. Four were bought by Stevensons of Uttoxeter in 1987; this one is seen in Burton-upon-Trent ten years later in a livery shared with Midland Red North.

In 1995–96 Northumbria took delivery of 20 Scania L113s with East Lancs European bodies. They were new in Northumbria's distinctive red, white and grey colour scheme, but were soon being repainted in Arriva's corporate livery as here in Newcastle in 1999 with Arriva North East.

Expansion at the end of the decade was slower than in the middle years, but Arriva did buy a few small operators, of which the best-known was McGill's of Barrhead, the original family-owned company, which was not connected with the major operator of the same name that would emerge in later years. It also bought the substantial London sightseeing operations of London Coaches, operated with 81 buses, most of them open-top double-deckers. The final Arriva acquisition came in 2000 in the shape of MTL, the former Merseyside PTE bus operation which ran 970 buses.

At the end of 2000 the Arriva fleet numbered 7,500 buses, covering the country from Kent to Clydeside with a strong presence in London, the Midlands and north-west and north-east England. ■

Vehicle policy

British Bus bought significant numbers of Dennis chassis; many were bodied by East Lancs, but there were other builders too including Northern Counties and Plaxton.

The vehicle policy adopted by Cowie and Arriva in the 1990s can best be described as varied. At different times it bought Volvo Olympians, Volvo Citybuses and Scania double-deckers. There were Scania single-deckers, too, along with Dennis Falcons, Lances and Darts. Bodywork came primarily from East Lancs, Plaxton and Wright.

Four of London & Country's 1989 Northern Counties-bodied Volvo Citybuses ended up with Arriva Midlands North via Bee Line in Manchester and Midland Red North. This is Birmingham in 2000.

◄ In the early 1990s Caldaire and its successor Westcourt bought 51 Optare Vectas for United Auto, Tees & District and Teesside, making them the biggest user of the Vecta, which was built on an MAN 11.190 chassis. They were 42-seaters. This bus was new to Tees & District in 1993 and is seen in Middlesbrough in 1999, running for Arriva North East.

▼ Northumbria's first new double-deckers were ten long-wheelbase Leyland Olympians with 80-seat Alexander R-type bodies, delivered in 1988. This 1999 view in Newcastle shows an Olympian in the ownership of Arriva North East.

In 1998 Arriva Scotland West received 15 Dennis Dart SLFs with Alexander ALX200 bodies. This was the former Clydeside 2000 business which had been taken over by British Bus in 1994.

Some of the first low-floor double-deckers for service in London were DAF DB250s with Alexander ALX400 bodies, with 123 entering service with Arriva in the winter of 1998–99. They had just 62 seats. On its London fleets an upswept cream band echoed the colour break on Arriva's corporate turquoise livery.

The growth of Arriva

Year	Company	Fleet size	Bought from
Drawlane/British Bus			
1987	Shamrock & Rambler	73	NBC (a)
1988	Midland Red North	248	NBC
	London Country South West	415	NBC
	North Western Road Car	340	NBC
	East Lancashire Coachbuilders		John Brown Eng (b)
1989	Crosville	436	ATL (c)
	Midland Fox	375	NBC MBO
	Speedlink Airport Services	41	Split from LCSW (d)
	Bee Line Buzz	260	Stagecoach
1990	Alder Valley (Guildford area)	50	Q Drive
1992	Crosville Wales	479	National Express
1992 Drawlane reformed as British Bus			
1993	Southend Transport	136	Local authority
	Colchester Transport	56	Local authority
	Liverline	51	Owners
1994	Stevensons	270	Owners
	Proudmutual	770	NBC MBO
	– Northumbria		
	– Moor Dale		
	– Kentish Bus		
	Luton & District	550	NBC MBO
	Clydeside 2000	347	Employees/L&D
	Derby City Transport	121	Employees/L&D
1995	Caldaire	400	NBC MBO
	– West Riding		
	– Yorkshire Woollen		
	– Selby & District		
	– South Yorkshire Transport		
	Maidstone & District	300	NBC MBO
	Star Line, Knutsford	45	Owners
1996 British Bus acquired by Cowie			

Year	Company	Fleet size	Bought from
Cowie/Arriva			
1980	Grey-Green	94	Ewer Group
1988	Hughes DAF, Cleckheaton	-	Paul Sykes Group
1994	Leaside Buses	523	London Buses
1995	South London	447	London Buses
1996	British Bus	5,200	-
	North East Bus	422	West Midlands Travel
	– United		
	– Teeesside Motor Services		
	– Tees & District		
	County Bus & Coach	230	West Midlands Travel
1997 Cowie renamed Arriva			
1997	London Coaches (sightseeing fleet)	81	London Buses MBO
1999	Nova-Scotia Travel, Winsford	40	Owners
2000	MTL	970	PTE MBO

- Only acquired fleets of 25 or more vehicles are included. There were other, smaller, acquisitions.
- MBO – management buy-out.

(a) Closed 1989.
(b) Sold to a group of investors, 1994.
(c) Parts of Crosville were merged with North Western and Bee Line in 1989–90; what was left was sold to PMT in 1990.
(d) Sold to National Express, 1991.

ARTICULATED BUSES: EUROPEAN-STYLE EXOTICA

In mainland Europe articulated buses swallow crowds. Boarding is fast, generally using three doors. Capacity is impressive, typically around 150. Comfort? Well, maybe not so good. British operators preferred double-deckers.

The first interest in articulated buses in Britain came from the South Yorkshire PTE. In the summer of 1977 Leyland provided the PTE with a left-hand-drive model built by its majority-owned Danish subsidiary DAB, which was tried in service in Sheffield, operating on trade plates. Further demonstrators were tried before the PTE ordered ten artics, five each from MAN and Leyland. The artics were 16.4m-long 60-seaters and were for a Cityliner service in central Sheffield where passengers would be making short journeys and would be unlikely to want to climb the stairs of a double-deck bus to get to a seat. They entered service in 1980.

The five Leylands had chassis built in Denmark by DAB with bodies built in Workington using Leyland National parts. Seven broadly similar buses, but with doors on both sides of the body, were supplied to British Airways in 1982.

The South Yorkshire articulated buses were withdrawn in 1982 The five MANs were then evaluated by City of Oxford and Midland Red West before being bought by Midland Red North where they entered service in Cannock at the start of 1984. All were withdrawn in 1987. One was scrapped and the other four were exported to Australia.

Two of the Leyland-DABs were used by McGill's of Barrhead and were then bought by Stagecoach and used by Hampshire Bus. The other three saw no further use as PSVs.

There was renewed interest in artics at South Yorkshire, and in 1986 a batch of 13 Leyland-DABs was delivered. These were built in Denmark with standard DAB bodywork. Ten were three-door 61-seaters for the City Clipper service which had succeeded the Cityliner in Sheffield. The other three were two-door 67-seaters, for operation between Rotherham and the shopping centre at Meadowhall. At the start of 2000 all were still owned by First Mainline, the successor to the PTE bus operation, although by the end of the year the three 67-seaters had been sold to the Bath Bus Company.

The biggest interest in artics in twentieth century Britain came from First, which in 1999 put 40 Volvo B10LAs into service, followed in 2000 by 30 Volvo B7LAs. All had Wrightbus bodies – Fusions on the 1999 buses and the revised Eclipse Fusion on those delivered in 2000. First predecessor GRT had experimented with a solitary artic in 1992, a Mercedes-

▼ The South Yorkshire PTE was the first British operator to express serious interest in articulated buses, taking delivery of ten in 1980. Five were Leyland DABs with bodywork built at the Leyland National factory in Workington.

The other five South Yorkshire artics were MAN SG192Rs. When they were withdrawn in 1982 they were tried by various NBC companies, ending up with Midland Red North which operated them between 1984 and 1987. This is Cannock in 1985.

A second generation of artics joined the South Yorkshire fleet in 1986. These were built in Denmark by DAB. This is a 1992 view in Sheffield.

Benz O405G with Alexander body. The later low-floor O405GN was operated in Birmingham by Travel West Midlands, with 11 delivered in 1999. These were complete Mercedes-built buses.

At the end of 2000 there were 95 articulated buses in service in Britain. In addition Stagecoach was running 13 Volvo B10M articulated coaches.

British artic fleet, 2000

Bath Bus Company	3	Leyland-DAB
First	10	Leyland-DAB
	40	Volvo B10LA/Wright
	30	Volvo B7LA/Wright
	1	Mercedes-Benz O405G/Alexander
Stagecoach	10	Volvo B10MA/Plaxton
	3	Volvo B10MA/Jonckheere
Travel West Midlands	11	Mercedes-Benz O405GN integral

▼ In 1981 Volvo was ready to sell articulated B10M coaches in Britain, with both Duple and Jonckheere expressing an interest in the concept. But when the government ruled that articulated coaches would be banned from the outside lane of three-lane motorways the project was shelved. However articulated coaches finally did appear in 1996, when Stagecoach evaluated 13 Volvo B10MAs on express services. They seated 71 passengers. This is one of ten bodied by Plaxton.

▼ First was the first operator to purchase large numbers of articulated buses for city services. Forty Volvo B10LAs with Wright Fusion bodies joined the First fleet in 1999 and were shared between Manchester, Leeds and Glasgow. The 15 buses allocated to First Manchester ran between Manchester and Bury, competing with the Metrolink rail service.

12
Beyond the Big Three

PALACE PLACE

By the year 2000 Britain's three biggest groups, Arriva, First and Stagecoach, were between them running 25,000 buses and coaches. That's more than the combined 1980 fleet strength of the National Bus Company and Scottish Bus Group.

But jump back ten years, and it was by no means clear that the industry would develop in this way. Indeed, after the upheaval of the NBC sell-off, the restructuring of SBG and the PTEs, and the early privatisation of several municipal operations, the bus world towards the end of the 1980s appeared to be settling into a different kind of order.

Admittedly, there were still skirmishes between rival companies; there were still periodic takeovers and municipal sell-offs; under-funded independent operators kept popping up; and the disposals of SBG and the PTEs were still largely in the future. All the same, new local and regional brand names were establishing themselves, and the future of the industry looked set to be a colourful and diverse one.

With the benefit of hindsight, it is easy to think of some of the developments in this period as having been short-lived; and some of them definitely were. But a few of the operators that emerged or refreshed their image around this time lasted for many years, and some survived well into the new century. If you were growing up in a town served by, say, Northumbria Motor Services or Bristol Omnibus,

▲ Most of the familiar company names revived in the 1980s were short-lived, but Brighton & Hove (harking back to the days of Brighton Hove & District) proved to have staying power. However, the management team that bought the company from NBC switched to Scanias for its double-deck fleet, and altogether 30 N112s and N113s were acquired between 1988 and 1990, all with 80-seat East Lancs bodies. This is a 1992 view; the following year Go-Ahead took over, but kept faith with the brand. The dot-matrix destination display was unusual for its time.

you could have been forgiven for thinking those companies and their vivid identities were fixed and immutable.

Those two operators' identities were eventually dropped by Arriva and First respectively, but it is worth remembering that by 1990 only Stagecoach had introduced a nationwide identity; the corporate look for Arriva and First only appeared in the late 1990s.

The following pages celebrate this substantial interim period, focusing on bus groups outside the big three – some of which stayed the course, and some of which soon disappeared – and on the privatised NBC businesses that were still independent companies in 2000. ■

◄ Between 1978 and 1989 the West Midlands PTE and its successor, West Midlands Travel, took delivery of 1,132 MCW Metrobuses. An example of the original version, new in 1981, is followed by a 1984 Mark II in Wolverhampton in 1990. The operation was privatised in the following year in a management-led employee buy-out. It was bought by National Express in 1995.

Go-Ahead

NBC's Northern General was one of the major urban operators in north-east England. It was privatised in a 1987 management buy-out and during the 1990s expanded in its home territory – and elsewhere in England. In the north-east it bought OK Travel, an established company which had almost trebled in size since deregulation and had a fleet of 200 buses. In the south it bought two former NBC companies from their management teams, Brighton & Hove in 1993 followed by City of Oxford in 1994.

Go-Ahead's most significant 1990s growth came in London, where it bought London Central in 1994 followed by London General in 1996. Between them they ran 1,100 buses. To these it would add the 200-bus fleet of Metrobus of Orpington in 1999. In 1997 it expanded on the south coast when it bought Brighton Borough Transport, giving Go-Ahead a virtual monopoly of local services in the Brighton and Hove conurbation.

Subsequent acquisitions meant that by the early years of the new century Go-Ahead had come to be seen as one of Britain's "big five" major bus operators, along with National Express (page 125). ■

▼ In 1992 Go-Ahead Northern adopted distinct liveries for each of its operations in north-east England. VFM Buses was based in South Shields and used the two-tone blue scheme seen on this 1985 ECW-bodied Leyland Olympian. It was unusual in being part of a batch with Cummins L10 engines at a time when most NBC Olympians were Gardner-powered. VFM stood for Value For Money.

◄ Wear Buses used two-tone green. Its operations were centred on Sunderland, the location of this view of a 1986 MCW Metrobus II. Northern General was the biggest NBC operator of Metrobuses, building up a fleet of 97 between 1980 and 1986.

➤ The new Northern operation retained red, the traditional colour of its Northern General forebear, albeit now in a stronger shade than NBC's. A new 40-seat Marshall-bodied Dennis Dart is seen in central Newcastle in August 1996. The Marshall body was a development of the original Duple Dartline body for the Dart.

◄ OK Travel was purchased by Go-Ahead in 1995. Among the vehicles taken over was this 1981 Leyland Leopard which had been new to Rhymney Valley. It had an East Lancs body. This is central Newcastle in 1996.

◄ The Oxford Bus Company, a rather catchier title than The City of Oxford Motor Services which was the company's name, was bought by Go-Ahead in 1994. In the winter of 1995–96 the company added 24 Volvo B10Bs with Plaxton Verde bodies to its fleet. This is a 1996 view in Oxford city centre. The adoption of the Verde name was an early and subtle bid by a manufacturer to promote the bus industry's aspiration to be seen as having green credentials.

▼ Go-Ahead bought two London bus companies in the mid 1990s, running 1,100 buses between them. Volvo Olympians were the preferred choice for its London operations. In 1997 London General bought 58 of them with 74-seat Northern Counties Palatine bodies. One leaves Putney Bridge Station in 1998, bound for North Cheam. Behind it is Fulham House, a Territorial Army centre on the edge of the Putney Bridge Conservation Area.

National Express

National Express was best known as the provider of coach services across Great Britain, and was privatised in a management buy-out in 1988. Later that year it made its first foray into bus operation, buying Crosville Wales, but this arrangement was relatively short-lived; Crosville Wales was taken over by Drawlane in 1992. This happened after the 1991 purchase of National Express by a consortium that included Drawlane, which was followed at the end of 1992 by flotation on the stock exchange.

National Express then expanded, buying Scottish Citylink in 1993. Its definitive move into bus operation came in 1995 with the acquisition of West Midlands Travel, the former PTE bus operation, which it rebranded Travel West Midlands. WMT brought with it County Bus & Coach in Essex and Westcourt in north-east England. Both of these were sold to Cowie in 1996. WMT had dabbled in the London bus market, owning Stanwell Buses in 1994–95, and in 1998 was back, briefly, in the shape of Travel London. This was sold to Limebourne in 2000.

The National Express group's most successful bus expansion outside the West Midlands came with the 1997 acquisition of Tayside Transport, soon renamed Travel Dundee. From that point onward its presence in the bus business remained remarkably stable, making it something of an anomaly in its world: a large publicly-quoted group with just two widely separated bus operations in Britain – one of which, Travel West Midlands, was among the largest in the country. ■

In 1999–2000 Travel West Midlands introduced 99 low-floor Volvo B7TLs. They had 74-seat Plaxton President bodies built at Northern Counties' Wigan factory, which had been taken over by Plaxton in 1995.

▲ (top) West Midlands Travel adopted this livery in 1990, using stronger colours than hitherto. This is a newly-delivered Volvo B10B with Wright Endeavour body in Wolverhampton in 1996.

▲ (above) National Express acquired West Midlands Travel in 1995 and introduced a brighter livery. It was usually red, white and blue but this bus was part of the Travel Your Bus fleet and has orange in place of red. The independent Your Bus company had used an orange, brown and white livery inspired by ex-Greater Manchester buses. in 1997 TWM took 20 Volvo B10Ls with Wright Liberator bodies, seven of which were allocated to the Your Bus fleet. Although the Liberator looks like the Endeavour in the previous photo it differs in being a low-floor model.

Caldaire

Caldaire quickly became one of the biggest of the emerging new groups and it was also one of the longest-lived, surviving for eight years. It was the holding company formed by the management team that bought West Riding and Yorkshire Woollen in 1987, and after buying United Auto in the autumn of the same year it had almost 1,000 vehicles. At the time this made it bigger than Stagecoach, with 700.

Although Caldaire seemed busy on numerous fronts, much of its activity involved splitting up and re-forming acquired businesses. But there was genuine expansion in Sheffield, where it created a new company, Sheffield & District, to compete with the PTE, and also in

the north east, where it acquired the linked businesses of Trimdon Motor Services and Teesside Motor Services, which ran 120 buses between them.

In 1992 the group sold its north east operations to a new company, Westcourt, set up by former Caldaire directors. This would be taken over by West Midlands Travel in 1994 and then sold to Cowie in 1996. In a final burst of expansion in 1994 Caldaire acquired the old-established Pontefract-based independent South Yorkshire Transport (not to be confused with the PTE-owned company of the same name), but then it sold out to British Bus in March 1995, by which time its fleet had shrunk to 400 buses. ■

▲ The Caldaire group replaced the NBC corporate look with a cream livery relieved by green for West Riding, blue for Sheffield & District and, as here in Huddersfield in 1990, dark red. This ECW-bodied Leyland Olympian had been new to Yorkshire Woollen District in 1984. Although this was still the company's name, Caldaire gave it a more modern brand, Yorkshire Buses.

➤ Green was the colour adopted for Caldaire's West Riding company. This is one of three Optare MetroRiders new to tiny sister-company Selby & District in 1995. It is seen in Wakefield in 1997, by which time Caldaire had sold out to British Bus (soon to become part of Arriva).

ATL

The ATL Group – the initials were those of founder AT Lavin – had a shorter life than Caldaire. It was associated with Carlton PSV, the Neoplan importer, and initially focused on coaching. It acquired the 60-vehicle coach fleet of Yelloway Motor Services of Rochdale in August 1985, then the following year bought National Travel East from NBC. It renamed this company SUT, the initials of Sheffield United Transport (once a coach operator in the city), but could not use the full name because the rights were held by rival coach firm Wallace Arnold.

Yelloway and SUT then branched out into local bus operations in Manchester and Sheffield respectively, using an assortment of second-hand vehicles. The group had high ambitions, and went on to acquire Crosville in March 1988, but both Yelloway and SUT were soon in trouble with the traffic commissioners because of poor maintenance of their elderly fleets, and ATL was forced to merge Yelloway with its Crosville business in late 1988 – an ignominious end for a famous name.

ATL disappeared in 1989. Crosville, with 436 vehicles, was sold to Drawlane in February. A small Leeds operation, Airebus, simply closed, while SUT's 58-vehicle bus operation in Sheffield ended up with PTE-owned South Yorkshire Transport, and National Express took over the remaining coach operations, plus the Carlton PSV dealership. ▪

Proudmutual

Proudmutual was one of the most stable of the emerging groups. It acquired Northumbria in a management buy-out in October 1987 and then bought Kentish Bus – previously known as London Country South East – in the spring of 1988. This gave it a fleet of around 500 buses.

Kentish Bus expanded into London, winning a number of London Transport contracts. These included one for a Routemaster-operated route, which saw RMLs being painted in Kentish Bus colours. When Boro'line Maidstone ran into problems at the start of 1992 Kentish Bus took over Boro'line's London contracts, along with 57 vehicles.

Proudmutual, now operating 770 vehicles, was bought by British Bus in 1994. ▪

▲ SUT was a subsidiary of the ATL Group, and operated local services in Sheffield between 1986 and 1989. Most of its buses were old and second-hand, but notable exceptions were a pair of Neoplan N416s. ATL owned Carlton PSV, the UK importer of Neoplan coaches, and thought it saw an opportunity to sell the N416 in deregulated Britain. Two were imported but found no buyers and so joined the SUT fleet. SUT's operations, including the unusual Neoplans, were taken over by South Yorkshire Transport in 1989.

▲ Unlike many contemporaries, Northumbria resisted compromising on the initial dramatic livery with which it was launched in the 1980s. The complex diagonal scheme looks immaculate on this Northern Counties-bodied Volvo Olympian, which is seen in Newcastle in 1996, two years after parent Proudmutual's acquisition by British Bus. The bus was one of eight new to Northumbria in 1994.

AJS

The AJS Group – the initials of Alan J Stephenson, chairman of NBC buy-out East Yorkshire Motor Services – owned two former NBC subsidiaries, purchased in conjunction with Parkdale Holdings, a property company. These were West Yorkshire Road Car and London Country North East. The group's fleet was 900 vehicles.

West Yorkshire had been a major player over a wide area for many years, but under AJS it was split into smaller companies. Parts were sold to Yorkshire Rider in 1989–90. Similar splits followed at London Country North East, and two of the resultant units, County Bus & Coach in Essex and Sovereign Bus & Coach's operations in Stevenage,

were then sold in 1990–91. That left AJS with the southern part of Sovereign, plus what remained of the former West Yorkshire business, namely local operations in Keighley and Harrogate and interurban services from Leeds to the east coast which were the responsibility of a new subsidiary, Yorkshire Coastliner. All of this was sold in 1991 to Blazefield Holdings, set up by two AJS directors, creating a new group with 300 vehicles.

East Yorkshire, which was not part of the AJS Group, survived intact, and would continue as an independent company for nearly 30 years. ■

◄ As privatisation loomed, West Yorkshire reverted to a remarkably authentic-looking version of its pre-NBC livery, suggesting a confident future for this large and long-established company. This 1979 Bristol VRT is seen in Leeds in July 1987. Five years later, West Yorkshire was just a memory.

◄ AJS subsidiary Keighley & District was formed in 1989 to take over part of the operations of West Yorkshire Road Car as it was slowly dismembered. For a short time it used this unusual grey livery (or chinchilla as the company described it), seen on an ECW-bodied Leyland Olympian which had been new to West Yorkshire in 1983. This is a 1990 view. Keighley & District was taken over by Blazefield in 1991.

Q Drive

Q Drive grew out of Len Wright Travel – a name synonymous in the early 1980s with top-specification coaches for pop groups. It moved into buses in July 1985 when it secured the contract to operate a London Transport service in the Hounslow area, for which it adopted the name London Buslines.

In 1987 it purchased from NBC the former Alder Valley North business, now named Berks Bucks Bus Co and trading as The Bee Line. A year later it acquired Alder Valley South from Frontsource, the original buyer. Alder Valley was thus re-united in common ownership just two years after having been split by NBC in readiness for privatisation.

After that Q Drive slowly contracted. In 1990 it sold Bee Line's 51-bus High Wycombe operations to City of Oxford, and the 50-vehicle Alder Valley operation in and around Guildford to Drawlane. That left it with 300 buses – a number halved in 1992 when it sold Bee Line's 56-vehicle Reading and Newbury operations to Reading Transport and Alder Valley's operations in Aldershot, Alton and Hindhead, with 90 buses, to Stagecoach.

Unexpectedly it augmented the surviving Bee Line business in Maidenhead and Bracknell in early 1993 by acquiring the 40-vehicle Slough operations of Luton & District, but in 1996 it sold its remaining bus operations with 180 vehicles to CentreWest. It made a brief return to buses in 1996–97, winning further LT contracted services through Limebourne, a coach business acquired in 1995, but these were short-lived; in the autumn of 1998 Q Drive called in the receivers. The Limebourne operation, however, survived under a management buy-out, and would eventually pass to Connex. ▨

▲ New to Alder Valley in 1980, this VRT passed in 1986 to the new Alder Valley South company, which was owned by Q Drive from 1988 to 1992. This is Basingstoke in 1988 and the VRT is in a livery that harks back to Aldershot & District, whose buses were two-tone green and cream until 1972 when the company was merged with Thames Valley to create Alder Valley.

➤ Among later batches of buses acquired new by Q Drive were ten Scania L113s with attractive Northern Counties bodywork, which arrived in 1995. This one is seen in Reading two years later, by which time the Bee Line operation had been purchased by First CentreWest.

Former NBC survivors

By 2000 most one-time NBC subsidiaries were part of one of the major groups – Arriva, First, Go-Ahead and Stagecoach. Just five survived in the ownership of their management buy-out teams, East Yorkshire, Trent, Southern Vectis, Wilts & Dorset and Yorkshire Traction.

The only significant expansion by East Yorkshire was the purchase in 1992 of Finglands of Manchester which ran 41 buses and coaches. To this it added the small Stagecoach Manchester operation – just 13 buses – in 1995 as Stagecoach cleared the ground in readiness to make a bid for GM Buses South. When Stagecoach bought GMBS in 1996 it sold the GMBS Charterplan business with 27 coaches to East Yorkshire. The following year East Yorkshire pulled out of coaching, selling that aspect of its business, including Charterplan, to one of its directors.

Trent expanded by taking over Barton Transport of Nottingham in 1989 (210 vehicles) and Kinchbus of Loughborough (57 vehicles) in 1998.

Southern Vectis, the main bus operator on the Isle of Wight, moved on to the mainland in the spring of 1987 when it set up Solent Blue Line to compete with Southampton CityBus. The business expanded later that year with the purchase of the

Southampton operations of Hampshire Bus from Stagecoach.

Yorkshire Traction was bought from NBC by its management in 1987 and in the following year bought sister NBC business Lincolnshire Road Car. It also took over old-established independent Gash of Newark in 1988. Gash briefly operated as a separate business but following issues around vehicle maintenance it was absorbed by Road Car in 1989. Yorkshire Traction consolidated its position in Lincoln in 1993 with the purchase of Lincoln City Transport. It was the successful bidder for one SBG company, Strathtay, which it took over in the summer of 1991. Expansion in the Sheffield area came with the purchase of Andrews, South Riding, Yorkshire Terrier and Sheffield Omnibus, purchased between 1992 and 1995. Between them these four operators ran over 150 vehicles.

Long-lived they may have been, but of the five surviving independents described here, three would be taken over by the major groups in the early years of the twenty-first century – Yorkshire Traction by Stagecoach in 2003 and Wilts & Dorset and Southern Vectis by Go-Ahead in 2003 and 2005 respectively. Then in 2018 Go-Ahead would also acquire East Yorkshire, leaving just Trent, or trentbarton as it liked to be known, as the sole former NBC business still independent in the 2020s. ■

Between 1988 and 1995 East Yorkshire operated ex-London Routemasters in the company's traditional dark blue colours on a service in Hull. After the Routemasters were withdrawn the blue livery was retained for the route, as seen on a 1998 Northern Counties-bodied Volvo Olympian.

◄ A batch of 11 Volvo Olympians with Alexander Royale bodies was purchased by East Yorkshire in 1995. They were unique among Royales in being lowheight bodies on long-wheelbase chassis. This bus has route branding for the service between Hull and the coastal town of Withernsea.

▼ In 1992 East Yorkshire bought Finglands of Manchester, a coach operator that had diversified into bus operation after deregulation. New vehicles added to the fleet included four Volvo Olympians with normal-height 74-seat Alexander Royale bodies. They were delivered in 1995.

◄ After buying 24 Volvo Citybus double-deckers in 1989 Trent decided to standardise on single-deck buses. The first, in 1991–92, were DAF SB220s with Optare Delta bodies, and these were followed in 1993–94 by 33 Volvo B10BLEs with 49-seat Northern Counties Paladin bodies. A Volvo leaves Derby in 1996, bound for Duffield, five miles to the north. The small sticker on the windscreen proclaims the bus is on a Rainbow Route, presaging the widespread adoption of distinctive route branding by the company.

► In Nottingham in 1998 a Plaxton-bodied Dennis Dart SLF in the Trent fleet carries Calverton Connection branding, with the letters CC in place of a route number. There's no indication that this is in fact a Trent bus, although bus users in the area would recognise the company's colours. As with many 1990s low-floor buses this one carries a promotional message on the lower side panels.

➤ Southern Vectis set up operations in Southampton under the Solent Blue Line name. New in 1991 were six Leyland Olympians with lowheight Workington-built Leyland bodywork. Students of Britain's vehicle licensing system will recognise the DL registration on this bus as being the letters allocated to vehicles registered on the Isle of Wight, where Southern Vectis was based.

After privatisation Wilts & Dorset became a loyal Optare customer. Between 1992 and 2000 all 210 of its new service buses came from Optare – 88 Solos, 59 Spectras, 49 MetroRiders, six Deltas and eight Excels. This is one of the first Spectras, based on a DAF DB250 chassis, in Bournemouth in 1993.

◄ Gash of Newark had started running buses in the 1920s, and had a long and honourable history. Its fleet in 1987 included this Leyland Titan, newly acquired from Greater Manchester Transport and photographed in Newark bus station. It was among the 39 buses in the Gash fleet when the company was bought by Yorkshire Traction in 1989.

NBC subsidiary Lincolnshire Road Car was bought by Yorkshire Traction in 1988. The company served a largely rural area, and the only new double-deckers purchased in the 1990s were eight Volvo Olympians with East Lancs bodies. Six were delivered in 1996 and were long-wheelbase models with 88 seats. The East Lancs body was a copy of Alexander's R-type, although long R-types featured a short bay within the wheelbase where East Lancs used equal-length windows which were shorter than those on its normal 9.5m-long body.

In 1995 bodybuilder Marshall of Cambridge attempted to break in to the complete small bus market with the low-floor rear-engined integral Minibus. At 8.5m in length and with up to 29 seats it competed with the smallest Dennis Dart, the Mercedes-Benz 811D and the Optare MetroRider. It was powered by a four-cylinder engine, either the Cummins B-series or the Perkins Phaser, and had an Allison gearbox.

Arguably the model was not strictly speaking a minibus (with a lower-case M) at all, since in UK terminology a minibus tended to have a maximum capacity of 16 to 20 passengers, and anything larger was regarded as a midibus. But the name certainly made the point about its relatively small size.

Marshall secured two fleet orders, 15 for London General and 16 for CentreWest. A further 18 were built for other operators before the project was abandoned in 1998.

On paper the concept looked good, but in practice the Marshall Minibus was one of the great failures of late twentieth century bus design. It was noisy, its four-cylinder engine created unacceptable vibration which made fittings work loose, and it was notably unreliable. The CentreWest buses, which were the last to be built, were described in Marshall publicity as having benefited from "a full development programme of improvements including noise control packages, engine cooling and a multiple of other modifications". But that clearly didn't impress CentreWest. All the Marshall Minibuses operated by London General and CentreWest were returned to their maker in 1999. Most were sold for further service in less demanding environments.

Marshall built 49 Minibuses. In 1999 ERF acquired the rights to build the Minibus chassis, presumably thinking that with its experience in truck production (and buses for Africa) it could do a better job than Marshall. However ERF was purchased by German manufacturer MAN in 2000, and that was the end of the Minibus.

The integral Marshall Minibus bore a strong resemblance to the company's Capital body for Dennis Dart SLF chassis. Fifteen Minibuses were supplied to London General towards the end of 1996, one of which is heading north on Putney Bridge in the summer of 1998 with Putney High Street in the background. All were returned to Marshall in 1999 and were then re-sold to a variety of small operators.

13
British bus building in decline

The Bristol factory closed in 1983. Workers remove the company's distinctive scroll from the wall at the factory entrance, closing a chapter in the history of British bus building.

The last two decades of the twentieth century brought mixed fortunes for Britain's bus and coach manufacturers. There were more losers than winners.

The long final phase of retrenchment at British Leyland's bus manufacturing had started in 1979 when the AEC factory at Southall closed, bringing an end to production of the Reliance single-deck chassis. There was considerable loyalty towards AEC among coach operators, and many switched to Volvo and DAF rather than buy Leyland's comparable Leopard. BL's nearby Park Royal body plant in the north-west London suburb of the same name closed in 1980.

While Leyland was struggling, some other bus manufacturers were growing. Dennis had re-entered the double-deck bus market in 1977 with the rear-engined Dominator. This was aimed at Leyland operators unhappy with that company's intention to concentrate on its integral Titan rather than on free-standing chassis which could be bodied by any bodybuilder. By the end of 1980 there were just over 100 Dominators in service. But having seen the error of its ways, Leyland introduced the Olympian chassis in that year, and this quickly became a best-seller, to some extent undermining Dennis's aspirations in the double-deck bus business. That said, Dennis did go on to build an eventual 1,007 Dominators, plus 2,106 three-axle export variants, Condors and Dragons, primarily for operation in Hong Kong.

MCW had launched the not entirely successful Scania-powered Metropolitan integral double-decker in 1973 and had replaced it with the much better-received Metrobus in 1977. This proved a winner with some big fleet operators, and there were around 850 in operation by the end of 1980 – an impressive figure which had risen to 3,887 when production ceased at the end of the decade.

The phasing out in the early 1980s of the government's new bus grant saw a drop in orders for all traditional manufacturers, and two

▲ Among the last true Bristol chassis to go into service was this ECW-bodied VRT, which joined the Bristol Omnibus fleet in mid-1981. By June 1989, when it was photographed in Stroud, it had passed to Cheltenham & Gloucester and was wearing this unusual Stroud Valleys livery. After VRT production ended Bristol went on to build around 1,000 Olympian chassis, but was then closed by its Leyland parent in 1983.

▼ After the Bristol factory closure in 1983 production of the Leyland Olympian chassis was transferred to Workington, where this one was built. Bodybuilder Roe closed in 1984, but re-emerged as Optare and produced 42 of these Roe-style Olympian bodies between 1985 and 1988. This is one of three late examples for former NBC subsidiary Cambus, and is seen in Cambridge in 1989. The batch was fitted with 70 high-backed seats and painted in NBC-style local coach livery.

more Leyland bus factories closed – the Bristol chassis plant in 1983 and the Roe body plant in Leeds in 1984. Roe would be given a new lease of life when it was taken over by Optare, a new company in which former Roe employees had a financial interest. When Bristol closed, production of the Olympian chassis was transferred to the Leyland National plant at Workington.

In some cases the retrenchment among traditional suppliers prompted manufacturers with related skills to try their hand at buses. Wadham Stringer of Waterlooville, a builder of ambulances and other specialist bodies, was a case in point. In 1979 it tackled the mainstream bus market with its Vanguard body, which sold in small numbers to bus operators, though its biggest customer was the Ministry of Defence. The company was bought by UVG in 1993, but this arrangement lasted just four years before the company called in the receivers. It was then acquired by Salvador Caetano (UK) which had some success building bodies on Dennis Dart SLF chassis.

New chassis manufacturing businesses appeared on the scene, too. In West Yorkshire the tiny Ward Motors company introduced the Dalesman coach chassis in 1982, followed by a rear-engined bus in 1983 – but shortly afterwards the company closed and the receivers were called in. Alternative Chassis Engineering (ACE) – in which the Ward family was also involved – started life in 1984, provocatively named the Albion Equipment Company (AEC). The use of the Albion and AEC names drew the ire of Leyland Bus, leading to the name change in 1985 to ACE. ACE lasted until 1992. Total production by Ward and ACE was around 30 chassis.

A shorter-lived entrant to the chassis market in 1983 was Quest 80 of Telford. It offered a range of chassis of which only one secured a significant order. This was a Ford-powered rear-engined 12m coach, and Ford operator Excelsior of Bournemouth ordered 20. Not all were built. Quest closed in 1985.

Two of the big names in coaching, Bedford and Ford, withdrew from the market in the mid-1980s as their traditional customers, family-run businesses, were switching to heavier-duty chassis better suited to fast motorway journeys and continental touring. Ford, which ten years earlier had been selling around 600 chassis a year, pulled out of the coach market in 1985. Bedford, which had been selling around 800 chassis a year in the 1970s and was owned by US automotive giant General Motors, withdrew from the UK completely in 1986.

The gradual collapse of Leyland continued in 1987 with the closure of Eastern Coach Works of Lowestoft. Production of double-deck bodies – by then ECW's speciality – was transferred to the Leyland National factory at Workington. In the same year Leyland Bus, as the business had been known since 1981, was bought by

The rear-engined Ward Dalesman GRXI was an attempt to sell city buses by a small Yorkshire chassis manufacturer. Only six were built, all for Darlington Borough Transport, and they entered service in 1983. They had Wadham Stringer Vanguard bodies. The GRXI model identification stood for Gardner, Rear-engined and – in Roman numerals – 11m long.

its management, who then sold it in 1988 – some would say with indecent haste – to Volvo.

Volvo quickly axed all Leyland's models except the Olympian, which was upgraded and fitted with a Volvo engine. Leyland chassis production had been moved from Workington to the Farington plant in Leyland in 1986. It would switch back to Workington in 1990, then that factory, too, closed in 1993 and Olympian production was transferred to Volvo's existing Irvine factory, where it would continue until 2000. Volvo had been building bus chassis in Irvine since 1975, when it had taken control of the Ailsa business.

MCW had done well with fleet orders for its Metrobus, but when it diversified was less successful. Its Metrorider small integral bus was well-judged for its market – a purpose-built alternative to truck-based buses from Mercedes-Benz and others – but proved troublesome in service. Its Metroliner coach range was short-lived, and Metrobus orders were adversely affected by the downturn in demand for double-deckers. MCW closed in 1989.

It was followed by Duple. The 1980s had been a difficult decade for the company. At the start there were quality problems with Dominant coach bodies. Then there were rapid model changes – Laser, Laser 2, Caribbean, Caribbean II, 320, 340, 425. On top of that there was growing competition from mainland European coach builders. Duple closed in 1990.

In 1980 Willowbrook of Loughborough was a company with a long history but a limited future. It secured orders from the National Bus Company for coach bodies on Leyland Leopard chassis in the early 1980s and built its last double-deckers, on Leyland Atlantean chassis for the Merseyside PTE, in 1982. Its main activity then became fitting new Warrior bus bodies to elderly Leopard chassis. The company faded away in 1992 but its name lives on in a retail park in Loughborough.

▼ In the early 1980s Duple's top model was the high-floor Caribbean. This is a 1983 Volvo B10M purchased by National Travel East for National Holidays European tours. National Travel argued that for continental touring it wanted coaches from a manufacturer that could provide effective support in the event of a breakdown, something it felt Leyland couldn't do. The Caribbean had been launched in 1982 for the 1983 season and although it was extensively revised in 1984 it was then replaced in 1985 by new 300-series models.

▲ Duple's main business was the production of coach bodies, but it built buses too. This is a Dominant bus, a model built between 1974 and 1987, and is unusual in being based on a short Dennis Lancet chassis. Ten of these were supplied to the Merseyside PTE in 1983.

▲ In 1987 the Dominant bus was replaced by the 300. Low Fell Coaches of Gateshead bought this Dennis Javelin in 1991. Low Fell had introduced a cross-Tyne bus service to Newcastle in 1982 in the face of strong opposition from the Tyneside PTE and existing bus operators. The PTE wanted cross-river travellers to take buses to Gateshead and transfer to the Metro. Low Fell was bought by Go-Ahead in 1992 but its identity was retained, as seen in this 1996 photograph. Duple built just over fifty bus bodies of this style.

▲ In the early 1980s MCW was having considerable success with its Metrobus and broadened its product range with the introduction of the Metroliner coach in 1983. The first five were supplied to NBC subsidiary East Kent in May 1983, and this one is seen on tour in the Lake District in June. While its styling probably didn't help – this version was replaced by a restyled and less boxy model in 1984 – the big obstacle in securing sales to small operators was the lack of a suitable service network and very real concerns about the Metroliner's residual value when the time came to trade it in for a new coach after a few years in service. MCW built a total of 42 Metroliner single-deck coaches.

Marshall of Cambridge had its ups and downs. Traditionally a builder of single-deck buses, the company had introduced its first double-decker in 1978. Between 1980 and 1984 it built 94 double-deck bodies for the South Yorkshire PTE and the municipal fleets of Bournemouth, Derby, Newport and Leicester, plus four stock Ailsas for Volvo and a demonstrator for Scania. After that it continued building single-deckers, primarily deregulation-era minibuses followed by the erstwhile Dartline body. This had been developed by Duple for the Dennis Dart, and was taken over by Carlyle when Duple closed. When Carlyle in turn closed in 1991 Marshall acquired the rights to the body. The company then developed it to fit the Volvo B6 and MAN 11.220 as well as the Dart, before introducing its new Capital body for the Dennis Dart SLF in 1996. The name was prophetic; most Capitals were sold to London operators.

Long-standing bodybuilder Northern Counties of Wigan called in the receivers in 1991 but was rescued by a management buy-out in 1992. In 1995 it was bought by Henlys, Plaxton's parent company. Two other old-established bodybuilders also survived, albeit with changes in ownership – East Lancashire Coachbuilders of Blackburn and Alexander of Falkirk. The latter was bought by the Mayflower automotive group in 1995. Mayflower then acquired Dennis in 1998 and set up a merger with Henlys, owner of Plaxton and Northern

Counties, in 2000, creating TransBus International. East Lancs was bought by a group of Jersey-based investors.

Dennis was one of the great success stories of the time with its popular Dart and its pioneering work in developing affordable low-entry single-deckers, most notably the Dart SLF. The letters indicated Super Low Floor. In the late 1990s it also launched what would become one of Britain's best-selling double-deck chassis, the low-floor Trident 2. To cope with growing sales in the UK and the Far East Dennis opened a new purpose-built factory in Guildford in 1990.

Another significant success was Wright of Ballymena which developed a strong presence in the British bus business. The breakthrough came in 1990 when it won orders from London Buses for bodies on Renault S75 and Dennis Dart chassis. But its real success came after the 1992 launch of a stylish new range of bodies, primarily for full-size single-deckers. These were joined and later superseded by the distinctive Millennium models, production of which started in 2000. The company had an enviable reputation for quality.

Optare, meanwhile, experienced various upheavals. In 1990 it was purchased by United Bus, the Dutch-based group formed in 1989 by the merger of DAF Bus and Bova. United Bus collapsed in 1993 and Optare was rescued by a management and employee buy-out. It

Ford was a strong performer in coach sales to independents, but in the 1970s it found a market for buses in the Scottish Bus Group, which bought almost 400, mainly for rural operations. This is a 1975 R1114 with 49-seat Alexander Y-type body in the Highland Scottish fleet, preparing to leave Fort William bus station in 1986 for the 45-mile trip south to Oban. Faced with declining sales Ford withdrew from the bus and coach business in 1985.

Wright's early buses were soundly-built using the Alusuisse system of aluminium extrusions but perhaps were lacking in style. In 1982 Maidstone Borough Transport took seven 61-seat Wright-bodied Bedford YMTs. This is a 1987 view, with Boro'line branding superimposed on Maidstone's previous brown livery. Wright grew to be a major bodybuilder; Bedford pulled out of the UK in 1986.

▲ Wright's success was built on a range of stylish single-deck bodies introduced in 1992. This attractive style was offered on a wide range of chassis; here is a 1998 Volvo B10BLE – on which the body was called Renown – with First Manchester.

▲ A collaboration between Renault and Northern Counties to sell the French manufacturer's PR100 city bus in the UK came to nought. Just five were built. Three were sold to Luton Airport in 1989 and the other two were demonstrators which ended up with Hornsby Travel of Scunthorpe. This bus was originally operated by London Transport and is seen in Scunthorpe High Street in 1997.

remained an independent business until 2000 when it was bought by North American Bus Industries. During this time it made a move towards becoming a builder of complete integral vehicles, first in 1990 with a reworking of the troubled MCW small bus (rebranded the MetroRider with an upper-case R), then with two low-floor models, the Excel in 1995 and the Solo in 1998.

Over two decades there was a remarkable reduction in bus and coach production in Britain. Factories were closed never to re-open in Birmingham, Blackpool, Bristol, London, Loughborough, Lowestoft and Workington, and bus production at Leyland in Lancashire came to an end after more than 80 years. In part, this retrenchment reflected the sharp decline in orders that dogged the bus and coach market in the post-deregulation years, but that is not the whole story. Operators still needed new vehicles, and in the place of the vanished manufacturers they were buying from elsewhere. In one case, Ballymena, that still meant the UK, but otherwise they looked increasingly to Belgium, Holland, Germany, Hungary, Portugal, Spain and Sweden. ■

Wadham Stringer introduced its Vanguard body in 1979. Most were sold to the British military or to local authorities as school or welfare buses, but the Vanguard did secure a few sales among mainstream bus operators. Newport Transport bought nine in 1983 on Scania BR112 chassis. The green dome in the background is the dominant feature of the former Newport Technical Institute.

➤ Wadham Stringer was bought by the Universal Vehicle Group in 1993. In 1995 UVG started production of the Urbanstar body for the Dennis Dart, then in 1997 adapted it for the low-floor Dart SLF. Around 80 low-floor Urbanstars were built before production ended in 1998 after UVG was taken over by Caetano. This 1997 bus is one of 14 bought by Marchwood Motorways of Totton and it was operated in Southampton on behalf of Solent Blue Line.

When coach services were deregulated in 1980 National Express became conscious of the need to promote its services more actively. This slightly risqué advert from the mid 1990s would surely have been unthinkable in NBC days.

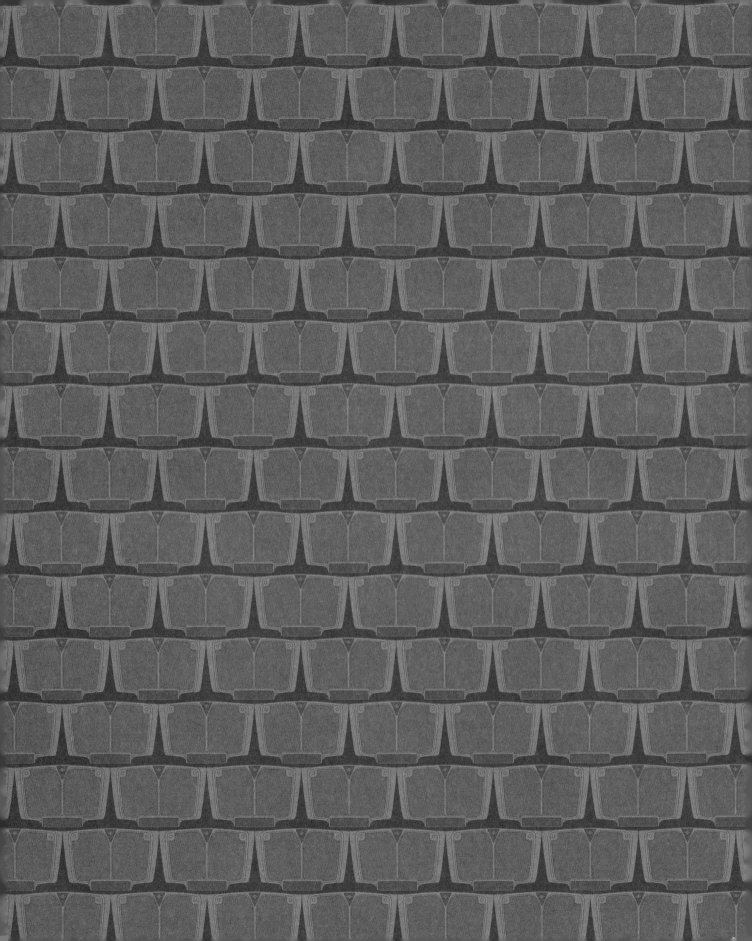